TURNING 18 & THE LAW

A COMPLETE GUIDE TO YOUR RIGHTS & RESPONSIBILITIES

• • • • • • • •

FREDRIC J. FRIEDBERG
Illustrations by
JOY F. FRIEDBERG

Schiffer Publishing Ltd

4880 Lower Valley Road   Atglen, Pennsylvania 19310

DEDICATION

To: Josh and Zach
Thanks for making your teen years a pleasure
for mom and I.

Other Schiffer Books By The Author:
Surviving Your Deposition, 978-0-7643-2681-3, $24.95
The Illinois Watch: The Life and Times of a Great Watch Company, 978-0-7643-2038-6, 6, $79.95

Copyright © 2010 by Frederic J. Friedberg
Illustrations Copyright © 2010 by Joy F. Friedberg

Library of Congress Control Number: 2010931637

Designed by John P. Cheek

Type set in Zurich BT/Minion Pro

ISBN: 978-0-7643-3608-9 (trade edition)
ISBN: 978-0-7643-3617-1 (professional edition)

Printed in China

Schiffer Books are available at special discounts for bulk purchases for sales promotions or premiums. Special editions, including personalized covers, corporate imprints, and excerpts can be created in large quantities for special needs. For more information contact the publisher:

Published by Schiffer Publishing Ltd.
4880 Lower Valley Road
Atglen, PA 19310
Phone: (610) 593-1777; Fax: (610) 593-2002
E-mail: Info@schifferbooks.com

For the largest selection of fine reference books on this and related subjects, please visit our web site at
www.schifferbooks.com
We are always looking for people to write books on new and related subjects. If you have an idea for a book please contact us at the above address.

This book may be purchased from the publisher.
Include $5.00 for shipping.
Please try your bookstore first.
You may write for a free catalog.

In Europe, Schiffer books are distributed by
Bushwood Books
6 Marksbury Ave.
Kew Gardens
Surrey TW9 4JF England
Phone: 44 (0) 20 8392 8585; Fax: 44 (0) 20 8392 9876
E-mail: info@bushwoodbooks.co.uk
Website: www.bushwoodbooks.co.uk

CONTENTS

● ● ● ● ● ● ● ●

This guide is not intended to serve as legal advice, but rather to prepare a person for what they might expect upon turning 18 years of age. This guide may not cover every area a new adult may encounter when they turn 18. If any reader has specific questions on the material covered in this guide, they should contact an attorney.

INTRODUCTION

• • • • • • • •

After my book *Surviving Your Deposition: A Complete Guide to Help You Prepare For Your Deposition* was published, my publisher, Peter Schiffer, discussed that there was a need to explain to teenagers what their legal rights and responsibilities are upon turning 18 years old. We concluded that there was a requirement for a plain written, direct guidebook to provide advice to new adults about their changing rights and obligations.

Having somewhat helped raise two sons that survived their teen years unscathed, and being a lawyer, we agreed that this would be a good subject for me to undertake. This book is a result of that request. The goal of this book is to set out clearly and simply the legal pitfalls an 18-year-old should be aware of upon becoming an adult in the eyes of the law.

This book focuses on the main areas of new rights and responsibilities an 18-year-old faces in the United States. In addition to explaining the laws and legal principles most likely to be encountered, the text cites numerous real life "Busted" anecdotes to help reinforce the points made in the text. Also provided are fun illustrations by my soul mate Joy Friedberg that hopefully help emphasize key items. Again, I thank my treasured assistant Linda Daugherty for preparing all of the drafts for this book.

Some of the subjects in this book are covered by many pamphlets prepared by State Bar Associations throughout the United States— they have done an excellent job addressing emancipation issues. Many of the efforts by these organizations are cited herein. In fact, it is suggested that this book be used in conjunction with any relevant material prepared by your State Bar Association.

To help emphasize important points in this book, many of the pertinent items are shaded within the text. Other key points that the reader should carefully consider, be aware of, or do, are in green print. Finally, other issues that should definitely not be done are set forth in red print. Once this book is read it can be quickly reviewed

5

at any time by merely going back and refreshing ones' knowledge by reading the shaded portions and provisions set forth in colored print. Parents, teachers, and related educational professionals should also read the book as a refresher.

It is the intention of the author, as well as that of the publisher that this book help new adults upon turning 18 to stay out of legal trouble, and be able to achieve their personal and professional goals without unfortunate repercussions.

I am sorry that Peter Schiffer did not survive to see the culmination of his idea for this book.

● ● ● ● ● ● ● ●

Chapter One
RIGHTS AND RESPONSIBILITIES ON TURNING 18

● ● ● ● ● ● ● ●

Rights and Responsibilities on Turning 18

Once you turn 18 you are an adult in the eyes of the law, your community, and school. Whether you are ready or not, mature or immature, responsible or irresponsible, you automatically acquire new basic rights. Immediately at age 18, without parental consent and in your own name, you have the following:

New Rights

- To enter into a legal agreement/contract (for example, to buy a car or rent property)
- To marry
- To be free of your parents' control
- To live independently from your parents
- To obtain medical treatment without the consent of your parents
- To vote
- To apply for credit in your own name
- To work most kinds of jobs
- To join the armed forces
- To make a will
- To hold a public office
- To own a gun for hunting (in most states after obtaining a license) [1]

Marked For Life

It is very important that you exercise these new rights maturely and responsibly as your failure to do so could result in your being punished as an adult and incurring life-long negative marks on your record that will be permanently open to the world to review and evaluate.

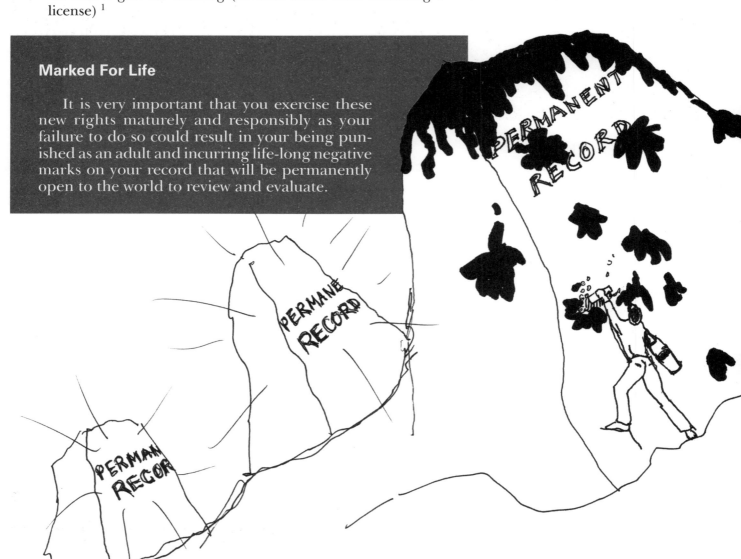

18, But

In most states, even if you are 18, you still cannot:
- Purchase or possess alcohol or alcoholic products until you are 21.
- Apply for a Concealed Weapon Permit.

With these new rights come new important responsibilities:

New Responsibilities

- Your actions are judged as an adult (juvenile law no longer applies)
- Your own support
- Repaying debts
- Paying for any injuries or accidents you cause
- Males must register for the draft
- Perform jury duty if called to serve

Emancipation

When you turn 18, you are considered "emancipated" in the eyes of the law. **Emancipation means you are "on your own."** Once you are emancipated, your parents are no longer required by law to support you; to tell you what to do; or to feed, clothe, or educate you.

But, if you are unable to work and support yourself, the law requires your parents to help as much as they can.[2]

Emancipated

You are considered emancipated when:
- You turn 18
- You are on active duty in the armed forces
- You get married
- A court orders your emancipation
- Your parents emancipate you in accordance with the law

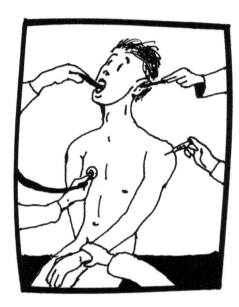

Consent to Medical Treatment

Once you turn 18, you do not need your parents' consent to seek and obtain medical, dental, or surgical treatment.

You can refuse medical treatment once you are 18, even if your death were to result from your refusal.[3]

Drug Treatment
Sexually Transmitted Diseases
Alcohol Abuse

At 18 you are able to seek your own treatment for drugs, sexually transmitted diseases (STDs), mental health, and/or alcohol abuse.

Common STDs

- Gonorrhea
- Human Papillomavirus Infection (HPV)
- Herpes Genital
- Pelvic Inflammatory Disease (PID)
- Chlamydia and LGV
- Syphilis
- Bacterial vaginosis
- Trichomoniasis
- Hepatitis (viral)

If you obtain treatment for an STD, the provider of the service cannot inform your parents or guardian without your consent. [4]

Of course, you will be responsible for the payment of those services.

Birth Control

At 18 you can obtain a prescription for birth control without parental consent. In 1965, the United States Supreme Court struck down the one remaining state law (in Connecticut) prohibiting the use of contraceptives.

Some Birth Control Methods

- Continuous abstinence
- Diaphragm
- Periodic abstinence
- Cervical cap
- Fertility awareness
- Shield
- Male condom
- Contraceptive sponge
- Oral contraceptives
- The "Patch" (Ortho Eura)
- The Mini-Pill
- The hormonal vaginal contraceptive (Nuva Ring)
- Copper T IUD (intrauterine device)
- Surgical sterilization
- Progestasert IUD
- Tubal ligation
- Intrauterine system or IUS (Mirena)
- Vasectomy
- Non-surgical sterilization
- Female condom
- Depo-Provera

You should consult with your personal doctor for the best method of birth control for your personal situation.

Teen STD Stats
1 in 4

In the U.S., one in four sexually active teens (more than 3 million teens) become infected with an STD every year. Some common STDs are chlamydia, gonorrhea, genital warts (also known as human papillomavirus [HPV]), and herpes. This is regrettable, especially since HPV is one of the leading STDs, and one for which a vaccine is available.[5]

19,000,000 per year

Nineteen (19) million new STD infections occur each year, almost half of them among young people ages 15 to 24.[6]

College Girls Alcohol Stats
60%

Sixty percent of college women diagnosed with a sexually transmitted disease were drunk at the time of infection.[7]

Teen STD Stats

One in two sexually active youth will contract an STD by age 25.

Forty percent (40%) of older adolescents surveyed by the Kaiser Family Foundation incorrectly believe that the contraceptive pill and shot protect against STDs and HIV.[8]

Teen Pregnancy Stats

The Guttmacher Institute reports that the United States has the highest levels of teen pregnancy among developed nations. This is hardly surprising, since nearly 75 percent of teenagers have had intercourse by the time they turn 20; only 15 percent report remaining virgins until the age of 21. Additionally, the Institute reports that teens in the U.S. are more likely to have sex before the age of 15, and to have more than one partner in a year, than teenagers in Sweden, France, Canada, and the United Kingdom.[9]

Virgins

Nationally, more than half of teenagers are virgins until they are at least 17 years of age.[10]

2,800 per day

Nationally, nearly one million young women under age 20 become pregnant each year. That means close to 2,800 teens get pregnant each day.[11]

4 in 10

Approximately 4 in 10 young women in the U.S. become pregnant at least once before turning 20.[12]

Teen "Pregnancy Pact"

A Massachusetts city is investigating an apparent teenage "pregnancy pact" that has at least 17 high school girls expecting babies, including many aged 16 or younger. This is four times more than last year.

A high school health clinic in the city of Gloucester became suspicious after seeing a surge in girls seeking pregnancy tests. Local officials said on Thursday nearly half of those who became pregnant appear to have entered into a pact to have their babies together over the year.

"Some girls seem more upset when they weren't pregnant than when they were," Gloucester High School principal Joseph Sullivan told *Time* magazine, which broke the news of the pact on its website.

Mr. Sullivan was not immediately available to comment. But local officials said at least some of the men involved in the pregnancies were in their mid-20s, including one man who appeared to be homeless. Others were boys in the school.

Carolyn Kirk, mayor of the port city 30 miles northeast of Boston, said authorities are looking at whether to pursue statutory rape charges. "We're at the very early stages of wrestling with the complexities of this problem," she said.

"But we also have to think about the boys. Some of these boys could have their lives changed. They could be in serious, serious trouble even if it was consensual because of their age—not from what the city could do but from what the girls' families could do," she told Reuters.

Under Massachusetts law, it is a crime to have sex with anyone under the age of 16.

"At the very least these men should be held responsible for financial support, if not put in jail for statutory rape as the mayor has suggested," Greg Verga, chairman of the Gloucester School Committee, told Reuters in a telephone interview.[13]

Jury Service

One of your new rights upon turning 18 is jury service. To serve on a jury you must:

- Be at least 18
- Be a United States citizen
- Not be too ill or disabled to serve
- Be able to understand English
- Live in the jurisdiction where you are called to serve.

If Called

If you are called to jury duty, you must reply to the court that contacts you unless you are excused for a special reason.

If you do not reply or give false or fraudulent reasons to avoid jury duty, your actions may constitute contempt of court. This is punishable by a fine or imprisonment.

News Flash

Recently in England a "4 year old girl has been called up for jury service."

Officials sent a letter to Beatrice Ball ordering her to attend a trial at Bristol Crown Court on June 5, 2007 reports *The Sun*.

Beatrice's mum Sam said: "She found it hilarious. Beatrice is bright for her age but this is ridiculous. [14]

Lists of potential jurors are usually developed from voter registration rolls and driver's license records.

Usually questionnaires are mailed to the potential jurors in advance to determine if they are qualified to serve on a jury.

Along with the questionnaire many courts give you a date to appear or a phone number to call to confirm your jury duty.

In other courts, when a jury is needed, the county clerk chooses names at random from the list of potential jurors. Those people are then "summoned" to appear at the courthouse at a certain time and date for jury selection. From this group the lawyers and/or judge select the jurors to serve on a particular trial.

You Are Excused

You may be excused from jury duty by some courts if you:
- Have a medical condition for which jury service could present a hazard to your health
- Are the primary caregiver of another person
- Are on active duty in the military
- Cannot secure childcare
- Will suffer extreme financial hardship
- Have a lawsuit pending in the same court
- Reside in a nursing home or institution
- Are a full-time student
- Are breast feeding a child and are not employed outside the home
- Are 70 years of age or older and are not medically able to serve
- Are a person who serves without compensation such as a volunteer firefighter, or a member of a rescue squad or ambulance crew
- Are a person whose services are so essential to the operation of a business, commercial or agricultural enterprise, that it must close or cease to function if you are required to perform jury duty
- Have served on a jury within the last year
- Are a peace officer
- Have been convicted of a felony or a malfeasance in office and your civil rights have not been restored.

You May Be Excused

Also, a judge can, at his/her discretion, excuse you from jury duty upon a finding of:
- Hardship
- Public necessity
- A bias that would keep you from deciding the case impartially (for example, if in a criminal case you strongly oppose capital punishment)
- An extreme inconvenience that your service would cause you
- Special circumstances that may excuse your service

Jury Pay

By law, your employer must give you time off for jury service (but your employer is not required to pay you for jury service in most states). Many employers, however, do pay your regular pay while you serve on a jury, or cap it after a set period.

Each county sets a rate of pay for jury service and some set an amount plus gas mileage reimbursement. [15]

While federal law does not, some state laws require employers to pay employees who are asked to serve jury duty. [16]

Jury Service: Be Aware

Jury staff of the courts do not ask past or prospective jurors for financial information such as credit card and bank account information or personal information like Social Security Numbers. Please do not provide this type of information to anyone claiming to be associated with the courts. Please contact your local jury office if you receive this type of request. [17]

Juror Basics

You do not need any special skills or legal knowledge to be a juror. All you need is an open mind and a readiness to work with the other jurors to make decisions. You also need to be impartial—in other words, your decisions must not be influenced by personal feelings and biases. [18]

Qualifications for Jury Service

California law says you are qualified to be a juror if you:
- Are a U.S. citizen
- Are at least 18 years old
  - Can understand English well enough to comprehend and discuss the case
  - Are a resident of the county that sent you the jury summons
  - Have not served on jury in the last 12 months
  - Are not currently on a grand jury or on another trial jury
  - Are not under a conservatorship
  - Have had your civil rights restored if you were convicted of a felony or malfeasance while holding public office

No one is exempt because of his or her job, race, color, religion, sex, national origin, sexual orientation, or economic status. [19]

Failure to Appear

If you are qualified and you have not been excused or had your service postponed, you must report for jury service. **You may only have to call a number or check a website to find out if you should report for jury service.** Any person who fails to respond may be fined up to $1,500. Jail time, in addition to the fine, is also possible. **Carefully follow the instructions on the jury summons and contact the court if you need help.**[20]

The Right To Vote

To be eligible to vote in most states you must be:
- At least 18 years of age
- A United States citizen
- A resident of your state for at least thirty (30) days before the election
- A registered voter at least twenty-nine (29) days before the election

Elections are generally held the first Tuesday in November. Under the Patriot Act, you must now show a photo identification when you vote. [21]

Where To Register?

You can usually register to vote at the Department of Motor Vehicles (DMV) office, certain public libraries, airports, shopping malls, and various public places. You can sometimes register online at your county clerk and recorder's office.

U.S. Citizenship

You are automatically a Unites States citizen if:
- You were born in the United States or one of its territories
- You were born outside of the United States but your parents are United States citizens, and at least one of your parents has lived in the U.S.
- One of your parents is a United States citizen and that parent lived in the United States for at least five (5) years, and at least two of the five years occurred after the parent's 14th birthday

Alien Students

If you are an alien student you should always have the following items in your possession:
- Your passport
- Your alien registration statement
- Evidence of school enrollment
- Evidence from school officials indicating you are maintaining the proper number of credit hours
- Evidence of your current address[22]

Other Citizens

If you are a lawful, permanent resident, always carry a photographic identification that indicates your status.

If you are a naturalized citizen, always carry your United States Passport.

Military Service

Once you turn 18 you no longer need your parents' permission to join the military.

After you turn 18 (if you are a male) you have thirty (30) days to register for the draft (Selective Service). You can also register up to 120 days prior to your 18th birthday. Your Selective Service registration must be kept updated until you turn 26.

Usually the Selective Service forms are mailed to your home, but they can also be obtained from any United States Post Office or online at http://www.sss.gov.[23]

Failure To Register

If you fail to register for the Selective Service, you are subject to fines up to $250,000 and/or up to five (5) years in jail.

Reasons to Join the Military

Recruiters state that the military will help pay for college and help pay off student loans. If you are in need of money for education, the military may be a viable option for you.

Soldiers do not just soldier. They have jobs within the military. In order for soldiers to be eligible for these jobs, they need to be trained. The training is usually extensive. This benefit may help open future employment opportunities for certain occupations such as a pilot, mechanic, or engineer. The training issued in the military may be a viable option for certain individuals.

There are other benefits that veterans are eligible for, including home loans, medical insurance, and educational funding. You may be eligible for these benefits for the rest of your life.[24]

UNCLE SAM WANTS YOU

Chapter Two
ARRESTS AND CRIMES

• • • • • • • • •

Arrests and Crimes

At 18 you are now judged as an adult in a court of law. Therefore, you must always be aware that your actions can result in felonies, misdemeanors, or infractions that can leave permanent, detrimental marks on your record, embarrass you and your family, and prevent you from attending the school of your choice or obtain the job or career that you seek. It cannot be emphasized strongly enough that one poor choice, one unthinking action, one drunken or drugged moment can adversely impact your life, career choices, or ability to earn a decent income.

Crimes are either felonies or misdemeanors.

Felonies are an offense where the penalty can be a jail term of one year or more.

Common Felonies

- Aggravated assault and/or battery
- Aiding and abetting/accessory
- Arson
- Bribery
- Burglary
- Cannabis cultivation
- Child abuse
- Child pornography
- Computer crimes
- Conspiracy
- Credit/debit card fraud
- Drug possession (over a certain weight)
- Drug trafficking
- Embezzlement
- Espionage
- Extortion
- Fraud
- Grand theft
- Identity theft
- Indecent exposure
- Insurance fraud
- Kidnapping
- Manslaughter
- Money laundering
- Murder
- Perjury
- Prostitution
- Pyramid schemes
- Racketeering
- Rape
- Robbery
- Securities fraud
- Sexual assault
- Stalking
- Tax evasion/fraud
- Telemarketing/fraud
- Theft/larceny
- Treason
- Wire fraud

Felony

Busted

Did you want a side of underwear with that order?

A teen accused of ordering from at least three fast food drive-thrus nude faces an indecent exposure charge.

David Gatton, 18, of Columbia City, was found in the parking lot of a McDonald's by a sheriff's deputy after police received a call that the teen had been nude when he ordered from his car at the Arby's drive-thru, police said.

"Maybe it was a way to enjoy the last of the warm weather," joked Capt. Brian Anspach of the Columbia City Police Department.[1]

If you are convicted of a felony, in addition to potential jail time and fines, you cannot:
- Work as a police officer
- Work as a lawyer
- Hold a public office
- Work in the securities and stock exchanges
- Vote
- Purchase firearms and ammunition
- Obtain a passport
- Obtain a Visa for international travel
- In some states, it is grounds for an uncontested divorce

Misdemeanors are any other criminal offense.

Misdemeanors vary from state to state. They are at times divided into classes with different degrees of severity of fines and/or jail time.

Infractions

Most states have offenses called infractions. They are usually viewed as a minor offense, minor violation, petty offense, or frequent citation. Sometimes they are also referred to as a:

- Violation
- Regulatory offense
- Welfare offense
- Combination (a petty violation of the law and less serious than a misdemeanor).[2]

Busted

Criminal trespass is a misdemeanor, but criminal damage to property is a felony.

It is homecoming season, and local high school students are keeping with tradition by pulling pranks. However, many property owners do not find the pranks funny, and they are calling the law.

The result is a number of teenagers being arrested on criminal trespass charges. The lucky ones are simply made to clean up their mess, but those who go a step beyond playful pranks may end up with felony charges, according to local law enforcement.

Within the last few days of September 2008, the Bulloch County Sheriff's Department made reports on at least seven incidents where someone threw rolls of toilet paper over trees and power lines, dumped shredded paper in yards, painted vehicle windows, shot homes with paint balls, and committed other offenses on private property.

...several teenagers were arrested on criminal trespass charges after they threw eggs and shot paint balls at a residence inside the Statesboro city limits...

"Criminal trespass is a misdemeanor," said Statesboro Police Capt. Scott Brunson. "But criminal damage to property is a felony." If the damage done to a home or vehicle is $500 or more, the offenders can be charged with criminal damage to property ...

Law enforcement officers have words of advice to teens who want to play pranks.

"Don't jeopardize your future over a silly prank," Brunson said. "You'll get a criminal record and somebody's going to get hurt."

"You'll wind up with a criminal record for being stupid," arresting officer McDaniel said. "And there is no need to cry when you're in the back seat of a police car going to jail. There's no need to blame your friends. Look into the mirror and you'll see who is to blame."[3]

Police Encounters

If you have the unfortunate experience of being arrested, you should know in advance how to behave, and under what circumstances you can be stopped by the police. Even innocent people at times can be subject to arrest, so it is important that everyone knows the rules and procedures when dealing with law enforcement officials.

If You are Stopped by the Police

- Always treat the police with respect.
- Even if the law officer has no suspicion of criminal activity, you may be stopped. If you are asked you must:
  - Supply your name
  - Supply your address
  - Supply your phone number
  - Respond with what you are doing
- If the officer thinks there is the possibility of criminal activity by you:
- You are free to leave unless you are being held in custody.
- If you are unsure, ask the police if you are free to leave, or if you are being held or placed in custody.
- If you are not being held or placed in custody, you do not have to stay to answer questions. You may stay and answer questions if you want to, but this may not be a wise thing to do.
- Be aware that anything you say to the police can be used against you in court.

Miranda Rights

If you are placed into custody, the police must read you your Miranda rights. Your rights are as follows:
- The right to remain silent.
- The right to be represented by legal counsel.
- The right to a lawyer if you cannot afford one.
- Anything you say can be used against you in a court of law.
- The right to have an attorney with you before questioned by the police.

No Miranda Warning

You should note that not receiving your Miranda warning is not a get of out of jail free card. If you are not read your rights (Miranda Rights) before you are interrogated in custody, the charges against you are not automatically dismissed. It just means the statements that you made to the police at that time may be excluded from evidence.

Any evidence that would not have been discovered without your original statement may not be admissible as evidence against you either. [5]

Police Encounters

There are three kinds of encounters with police officers:
- **Consensual Stop.** If a police officer stops you, the officer can ask you some general questions.
- **Investigatory Stop.** When an officer of the law has a reasonable suspicion that:
  - A crime has been committed.
  - A crime is being committed.
  - A crime is about to be committed.
- **An Arrest.** If a police officer has probable cause to think a crime was committed and that you committed the crime. [4]

Lawyer Contact

It is better to be safe than sorry and ask for legal representation at the outset. It would be advisable for you to be aware of the name and number of a trusted lawyer in advance, in the event you are ever in this situation. If you have a family lawyer or a lawyer who may be a friend of the family, you should always be aware of that person's contact information if you are ever in need of legal advice, or help getting out of jail on short notice.

Lack of Usable Evidence

Sometimes the lack of usable evidence can lead to a dismissal of your charges, but there is no automatic dismissal if your Miranda rights are not read. [6]

If You are Arrested

It is important for you to behave properly, responsibly, and appropriately at all times, so that you do not get arrested. But if you are arrested, you should be aware and prepared for the procedures and processes you will go through. If you are arrested, you will be searched, handcuffed, and taken to the police station. This is the standard procedure the police follow. Sometimes this can occur in very public and embarrassing locations, such as at school or at social events.

Arraignment

After arrest, you must be taken before a judge or magistrate without "unnecessary delay." This usually takes place within twenty-four (24) hours of your arrest.

At the Arraignment

The arraignment takes place in a courtroom in front of a judge, where you are formally charged for your crime. At that time you must plead guilty or not guilty.

Guilty Plea

If you plead guilty, you will be sentenced for your crime by the judge.

Not Guilty Plea

If you plead not guilty, the judge will then schedule your trial. At your trial, the prosecution must prove your guilt beyond a reasonable doubt.

Before You State Your Plea

- Make sure you fully understand what you are charged with.
- Understand your legal rights.
- If you ask, the judge will explain the proceedings.
- It is best to consult with a lawyer before you file your plea. A lawyer will be appointed to represent you if you cannot afford one. If you or your family has a lawyer, call that person to either advise you or recommend an attorney to do so.

Bail

Unless special circumstances exist, you will be released on bail after your arrest. The judge sets the amount of your bail. Bail is money you pay to the court to guarantee that you will attend all court hearings in your case and the trial. If you violate your condition of bail, you will forfeit this money and may be placed in jail. In some instances, the judge may set special restrictions on your bail such as preventing you from traveling out of state.

Before Trial

You should actively assist your lawyer in gathering evidence and witnesses to present in your defense in court. Make certain that your lawyer possesses all the necessary information pertaining to your violations, as well as any other factor about your history so your attorney is not surprised at trial or when dealing with the prosecutors.

There is more than one way to get arrested. Now police do not have to catch you in the act. There are security cameras located in more and more places, so it is difficult to commit a crime that remains unrecorded in many public places. Surprisingly, some not very bright people voluntarily post proof of their crimes on the Internet.

You should note that local law enforcement troll the Internet for evidence of criminal activity. Unfortunately, many very foolish teens make police work very easy.

Right to a Jury Trial

Any violation/crime that may subject you to more than six (6) months in jail triggers the right to a jury trial.

Juvenile Court

In almost all states (except Alabama and Nebraska), if you are 18 you are an adult and cannot go to juvenile court. You can also be tried and punished as an adult before you turn 18 under certain circumstances. The closer you are to 18 the less likely your case will be heard in juvenile court.

Other factors that may impact this decision are:
• Not living at home
• Having graduated from high school
• Working
• Being almost 18

At Trial

The prosecutor will present a case against you; your lawyer will present your defense. The judge or jury will evaluate all evidence and determine if you are guilty or innocent.

Busted

Police have come a long way since nailing wanted posters on the wall at the post office...

Detectives now put surveillance video of suspects on YouTube.

Nearly everyone who uses the Internet knows about YouTube. It's a site where you can upload a video and instantaneously it can be viewed anywhere around the globe. Now police are using this new technology. [7]

Not Guilty Verdict

If the judge or jury decides you are not guilty, all charges pending against you will be dropped and your case will be dismissed.

Guilty Verdict

If you are found guilty, the judge imposes punishment. The possible punishments are:
• Fine
• Probation
• Jail Time
• Community Service
• Restitution to the Victim

Appeal

You can appeal your verdict if you can properly claim the ruling or court proceeding was erroneous.

Finding a Lawyer

The best way to find a good lawyer is by obtaining a recommendation from a friend or relative. It is best to find a lawyer that specializes in or has good experience in the subject of your crime. The names of lawyers are listed on the Internet for different geographic areas and specialties. But a personal recommendation is the best referral.

If you do not like the lawyer you first meet with, find another one. Anything you discussed with the lawyer you first met must remain confidential unless you grant express permission for it to be disclosed.

If Stopped

Remember, if you are stopped by the police:
- You do not have to consent to a search.
- If you do not consent to a search, do not interfere with any search that may be conducted.
- If the police proceed with a search without your consent, ask the officer to note in his/her report that you did not consent to the search.
- If you consent to a search, be aware that anything the police find can be used as evidence against you.

Remember

If you cannot afford a lawyer, one will be appointed for you by the court.

Searches and Search Warrants

Searches

Always remember that if stopped by a police officer, even if you are asked to consent to a search, or are being pressured to consent to a search, you have no obligation to consent.

Search Warrant

As a general rule, the police must have a search warrant before searching a person or place.

A search warrant must be issued by a judge. The judge bases his/her decision on sworn testimony, usually from the police, that establishes probable cause that something unlawful has or will occur.

NOTE: In certain situations, a police officer does not need a search warrant. For example:

- If you consent to a search, you and your property may be searched (including your car, backpack, etc.).
- If the police have a reasonable belief that you are carrying a weapon, they may frisk you or search certain parts of the vehicle you are in.
- A search warrant is not required if you are arrested lawfully. In that case, police are free to search you and the area immediately near you. This includes your car (inside and out) and your trunk.
- If an emergency situation exists, or the police reasonably fear that evidence may be destroyed or removed, police may conduct a search without a warrant and there is not sufficient time to contact a judge.

If You are Arrested

If you are arrested, **DO NOT**:
- Resist
- Struggle with the police
- Fight
- Curse
- Argue
- Be confrontational

Even if you think the police are mistaken, do not do any of the above!

If you are arrested, **DO**:
- Provide your name, address, and phone number.
- Answer any questions the police ask, but ANYTHING you say may become part of the official record and can be used against you in a court of law.

If Arrested

- If you are arrested, you have the right to call a lawyer or a family member for advice.
- Police cannot force or threaten you to answer questions.
- The police cannot offer you a break or leniency in exchange for a statement from you.
- You are not free to leave if the police put you under arrest.
- The police must read you your Miranda Rights (please see page 20) before you can be questioned.

DO NOT be disrespectful, rude, or a wise guy to a police officer, even if you are completely innocent of the conduct you are being questioned about.

Arrests Without a Warrant

There are situations when the police can make an arrest without a warrant. For example, if:
- The police observe you attempting or committing a crime, or
- A reliable informant provides reasonably sound information to the police regarding a felony crime and you committed that crime, and if time permits, the police verify the information, or if time does not allow, the police should be reasonably certain that the information is valid, or
- The time spent obtaining a warrant would permit you to escape, or evidence to be lost, and
- The officer has probable cause for an arrest.

Busted

This is an instance where police noted that an illegal activity was taking place and went to a judge to have a search warrant issued to investigate the matter lawfully so that the evidence obtained could be properly used in a court of law.

A couple of Penn State students might be getting an "A"—if they were taking botany.

But they face prison time, for having an indoor pot garden. Police charge students Jared Gagne and Patrick Kelly, and recent grad, Kimberly Jasorka, had nearly 350 marijuana plants growing in an Altoona apartment.

Authorities say the suspects didn't live in the place, but just used it as a so-called "grow house." The plants were found after firefighters answered a false alarm in the building.

Officers then obtained a search warrant. Prosecutors put the street value of the weed at more than a half million dollars. [8]

An arrest without a warrant can also be made when a valid search occurs that reveals evidence that leads to the arrest. Also, evidence observed, or in "plain view," can substantiate probable cause for an arrest. However, there are exceptions to what constitutes "plain view," and most of those exceptions regard the Fourteenth Amendment of the United States Constitution—right to reasonable expectation of privacy. For example, your right to expect privacy is personal, so you may be at any location and have a right to expect privacy so long as the "place" is not of such a nature that reasonable people would not expect privacy.

Arrests: Illegal Search

Law Enforcement: Illegal Search Kills Prosecution in Largest Heroin Bust in California History.

Two Mexican brothers arrested in the largest heroin seizure in California history walked free…after federal prosecutors in San Diego dropped the charges against them. Prosecutors had little choice because a federal judge ruled…that police had violated the Fourth Amendment's ban on warrantless searches and threw out the evidence against them. Two others arrested in the case have already pleaded guilty and are awaiting sentencing.

At the time of the Valentine's Day bust, Immigration and Customs Enforcement (ICE) nearly dislocated their shoulders patting themselves on the back for uncovering what they described as a major heroin, methamphetamine, and marijuana trafficking operation. But their eagerness to search and make arrests eventually cost them the case.

It all started when ICE agents at the San Ysidro border crossing found a car with nearly 12 kilos of Mexican heroin hidden inside. The driver was allowed to continue to his destination in Anaheim under ICE surveillance. The driver met with another man, then drove to an Anaheim house and pulled into the garage. Without waiting for a search warrant, ICE agents entered and searched the house, arresting six people and seizing 121 pounds of heroin, 34 pounds of marijuana, and 3 pounds of methamphetamine, along with about $3,500 in cash.

Attorneys for the two Mexicans argued in court papers that the men had been staying at the Anaheim home and had a "reasonable expectation to privacy" guaranteed by the Fourth Amendment. They also argued that there was no threat to officer safety or that the evidence would be destroyed if ICE waited to get a search warrant.

Federal prosecutors argued that agents had no time to obtain a search warrant and that the drugs and the driver who led agents to the house were at risk, but US District Court Judge James Selma was not buying it. He instead ruled for the defense, holding that the search was unconstitutional and that the evidence derived from that search—the seized drugs—could not be admitted in court. [9]

Supreme Court Loosens Law on Illegal Searches "Honest Mistakes"

The United States Supreme Court pulled back on the "exclusionary rule" Wednesday, January 14, 2009, and ruled that evidence from an illegal search can be used if a police officer made an innocent mistake.

The 5-4 opinion signals that the court is ready to rethink this key rule in criminal law and restrict its reach. It will also give prosecutors and judges nationwide more leeway to make use of evidence that may have been seen as questionable before.

Chief Justice John G. Roberts Jr. said the guilty should not "go free" just because a computer error or a misunderstanding between police officers led to a wrongful arrest or search.

He said good evidence, even if obtained in a bad search, can be used against a suspect unless the police deliberately or recklessly violated his rights.

The exclusionary rule was applied to state and local police in 1961, and its aim was to deter officers from conducting unconstitutional searches of homes, cars, and pedestrians. Usually, it means that illegally seized evidence must be excluded.

But in Wednesday's opinion, Roberts said that "the benefits…must outweigh the costs." And there is nothing to be gained, he said, by throwing out evidence when officers make honest mistakes. [10]

Busted

You should carefully monitor and think about all possible implications when you interact with the police.

When you've just asked a cop for a lift, it might not be a good idea to bring a marijuana pipe along for the ride.

Christopher Lanzarotta, 18, watched as about a dozen friends got arrested on underage drinking charges at a house party in the early hours of September 2, 2007, Orland Park police said.

Then Lanzarotta...requested a ride to the Orland Park police station so he could bail out his friends. Officer Andrew Boblak agreed to give Lanzarotta and two friends a ride, and the group walked to Boblak's cruiser.

Lanzarotta brought along a massive duffel bag, perhaps not remembering it contained a multicolored, elephant-shaped glass pipe, police said.

Boblak asked to "quickly" search the bag to make sure it didn't have any weapons in it before the men entered the vehicle, according to police.

Lanzarotta complied, saying the officer was free to look in the bag because he wouldn't find anything.

But when Boblak looked in the bag, he saw the pot pipe in the duffel's side pocket, police said.

At that point, police no longer were doing Lanzarotta a favor by giving him a ride to the station. He was arrested and he has been charged with possession of drug paraphernalia, a misdemeanor. [11]

Torts

A tort is a legal term for certain injuries, accidents, or damages that you cause that can result in you being sued, even if it was an unintentional act on your part.

Some Common Torts Are:

- **Assault:** unlawfully attempting or threatening to touch or hurt another person (no actual touching is required).
- **Battery:** intentionally touching someone without their consent (actual touching is required).
- **Negligence:** breach of a duty of care owed by you to another.
- **Negligent Driving:** if you injure someone or damage their property while driving negligently.
- **Trespass:** entering onto someone's property without permission.
- **False Imprisonment:** preventing someone from leaving somewhere (e.g., a room, car, etc.)
- **Nuisance:** interfering with someone's use or enjoyment of their property.
- **Defamation:** the unlawful written attack (libel) on a person, or by spoken word (slander) that damages their name, reputation, or business. [12]

Arrest Record

A very important distinction for you when turning 18 is the status of your arrest record (a list of all of your legal offenses).

As a minor (in many instances) the law protects those under 18 by not making their "arrest records" public by keeping them under "seal."

When you turn 18 that is no longer the case; your arrests at 18 years of age or older are open to the public. Violations on your record could prevent you from accomplishing many of your personal goals such as attending college, seeking employment, obtaining a security position and certain positions in the military, or, until very recently, enlisting in the military.

Stay Under Control

You must always monitor your behavior and actions, as one reckless or careless unthinking act could damage you for the rest of your life.

Ignorance Of The Law

It is true that if you do something wrong that is illegal you can be found guilty whether you knew it was against the law or not.

Busted

Just because you are not aware of the existence of a law, does not excuse you from unintentionally violating that law.

An 18-year-old from Carlisle, Pennsylvania, has been charged with a felony under Pennsylvania's wiretap statute for videotaping a police officer during a traffic stop.

Brian D. Kelly didn't think he was doing anything illegal when he used his video camera to record a Carlisle police officer during a traffic stop. Making movies is one of his hobbies, he said, and the stop was just another interesting event to film…Kelly, 18, of Carlisle, was arrested on a felony wiretapping charge, with a penalty of up to 7 years in state prison…Kelly is charged under a state law that bars the intentional interception or recording of anyone's oral conversation without their consent.

One might think that the statute wouldn't apply to taping of public officials discharging their official duties in public places, but apparently that is not the case. Putting aside issues of whether civil liberties interests are best vindicated when there is rigorous oversight of those in power, this situation should provide a cautionary tale to video bloggers, podcasters, and others who gather news by recording video and audio or just audio in Pennsylvania. [13]

False Police Reports

Never file a false police report—doing so can be a crime. It will be viewed as a serious crime if you file false police reports that divert law enforcement resources from the pursuit of real illegal activity, plus it subjects all those involved to risk of injury.

Do not:
- Lie to a police officer
- Call in a bomb scare
- Call in a false fire alarm
- Commit perjury (not telling the truth under oath in court)[14]

Busted

Do not file a false police report.

A 19-year-old man from the state of Washington was arrested recently and faces numerous felony charges, including those involving illegal computer access of Orange County's 911 System, according to a news report posted on the NBC Web site.

Snohomish County resident, Randall Ellis, is believed to have gotten into Orange County's 911 System and placed a false report of a fatal shooting and threats at a couple's Lake Forest residence. Ellis was 18 years old when he allegedly pulled this out-of-state prank, reports the article. Ellis' actions reportedly resulted in a SWAT team being dispatched to the Lake Forest home and causing the couple to be put in harm's way. Authorities also believe Ellis to be responsible for more pranks in other states that were also 911 response related.

Prosecutors are obviously taking this prank very seriously. Ellis is currently being held without bail and Deputy District Attorney David Demurjian is promising to seek a bail amount of at least $500,000. Ellis, if convicted, could be looking at spending up to 18 years in prison.

People tend to pull such pranks possibly with a false sense of security and the belief their actions will be untraceable. But that almost is never the case. Farrah Emami of the D.A.'s office points out in the article that the origin of Ellis' false report was traced back using forensic computer technology by the investigators from the district attorney's High Tech Crimes Unit and sheriff's investigators.

High tech or computer crimes are serious offenses. Those alleged of hacking into bank and credit card accounts and other databases containing people's private information stand to face many years in state or federal prison—depending on who indicts the suspects...[15]

Terrorism

The September 11, 2001, terrorism attacks on the United States resulted in many legal changes. A number of these changes involved immigration laws. The passage of the Patriot Act and other security laws now requires citizens and aliens of many countries to register with the Immigration Naturalization Service (INS) and be photographed and fingerprinted.

Some of the changes resulting from the Patriot Act are:
- Broad surveillance methods (many are without consent)
- Physical searches
- Aliens must always carry documents that prove they were lawfully admitted for permanent residence in the United States. (Please see page 16)
- Alien students from a country designated as a security threat should check with their schools to determine whether they are required to register.
- Every alien who is now in the United States that is fourteen (14) or older who has not been registered and fingerprinted and remains in the United States for thirty (30) days or longer must apply for registration and be fingerprinted within thirty (30) days of arrival into the United States. [16]

Chapter Three
SHOPLIFTING

● ● ● ● ● ● ● ●

Shoplifting

Shoplifting is not just walking out of a store without paying for goods. Shoplifting includes any form of deception where you do not pay the asking price of the merchandise.

Shoplifting examples:
• Switching price tags
• Modifying merchandise labels
• Consuming food and concealing the wrappers
• Wearing articles of clothing and concealing the tags
• Walking out of a store without paying for goods
• Leaving a restaurant without paying the bill[1]

Avoid the temptation that almost all of us face at one time or another to slip something into our pocket when no one is looking in a store. Shoplifting (stealing from a store) is a crime. Nowadays, with the use of motorized video cameras and surveillance equipment virtually everywhere, you can never assume that no one is watching. Stores are tired of being ripped off, so they are much more aggressive in their surveillance and prosecution of offenders.

Shoplifting Advice

Ron Garcia, leader of the Asset Protection Program at a Mervyn's store in Tucson, Arizona said, "When you are a teenager, you really don't think about how much a $10 item can affect your future. If you get caught, stores typically show no mercy. That criminal record will be with you the rest of your life. It isn't worth it."

Shoplifting seems easy to get away with, but the time you get caught is when you least expect it. And you may have to get caught to learn your lesson.[2]

Felony

You may be charged with a felony in some states if you:
• Shoplift any item priced $100 or more
• Alter the price of an item
• Misrepresent the price
• Conceal the goods
• Switch labels on an item to get a better price.[3]

Second Shoplifting Offense

In most states, if you are charged with a second shoplifting offense, regardless of the price of the item you steal, you will be charged with a felony.

Do Not Help

If you help another person steal or shoplift and do not take anything yourself, you may be subject to the same penalties, depending on the circumstances.

Penalties

In most states, it is a petty theft misdemeanor if you shoplift an item that is valued at less than $300. In some cases, a first offense can be reduced to an infraction; if so, this would eliminate any criminal record.

If you shoplift an item of greater value, your crime can be classified as a grand theft or larceny felony charge.

Shoplifting Stats

Law enforcement professionals estimate that approximately ninety percent (90%) of the U.S. population will commit the crime of shoplifting at some point in their lives.[4]

Busted

If you are foolish enough to shoplift, you better wear a belt and suspenders.

A teenager arrested for shoplifting had filled her pockets with so many items that her pants dropped to her ankles as she tried to run out of the store, police said.[5]

What Happens to Shoplifters?

Getting caught shoplifting can be a lot more serious than you may think. Some of the things that can happen to you are:
- You may be arrested and paraded through a store in handcuffs.
- You may face charges for thefts.
- You may be banned from stores or malls.
- If you have been arrested for shoplifting—especially if you have multiple violations—you may end up with a criminal record.
- Even if you are not prosecuted, your name can end up on a national database that some companies search before making hiring decisions.[6]

Shoplifting Can Be Grand Theft

In California, for example, grand theft is committed when the money, labor, real, or personal property taken is valued at more than $400. Grand theft can be charged as a misdemeanor or felony and is punishable by up to one year in county jail or sixteen months in state prison. Depending on the value of the goods stolen, shoplifting can be considered either petty theft or grand theft.[7]

Busted

A family affair…

A grandmother, her daughter, and some of her grandchildren tried to steal $900 worth of merchandise from a Target store in Lodi, 35 miles south of Sacramento, police Officer Misty Smith said.

The family's alleged shoplifting spree earlier this week was captured by surveillance video, which police say showed them cutting open boxes and hiding MP3 players, digital cameras, DVDs, jewelry, and sports equipment in purses, bags, and a backpack.

An 8-year-old and a 5-year-old were among the family members detained.

"The 5-year-old actually had a pack of gum. A small item but we could see where her life was heading because she thinks more than likely this is a normal way of life, this is what you do," said Dale Eubanks of the Lodi police.

Linda Robinson, 59, and her 36-year-old daughter, Anna Fernandez, were charged Wednesday with burglary, grand theft, vandalism, and contributing to the delinquency of a minor. They were released from jail. If convicted, each could face eight years in prison. Fernandez's teenage sons, 17 and 14, were arrested on suspicion of grand theft and will face charges in juvenile court, authorities said. Another teen not related to the family also was arrested.

The two children were released to relatives and will not face charges.

It was not immediately clear if the family had a lawyer.[8]

Chapter Four
WEAPONS AND GUNS

● ● ● ● ● ● ●

In most states you must be at least 18 years old to possess or own a handgun. But you should think long and hard as to why you would need a handgun and would want to own one. Realistically, there are virtually no valid reasons for an 18-year-old to own a handgun. If you want one to show off to your friends, to post pictures of yourself with on MySpace or Facebook, or for protection at a high school football game, then unfortunately it is clear that you are not mature enough or intelligent enough to own one.

Protection

You should not carry a weapon for protection. It is against the law to attack someone with a dangerous weapon or to have a dangerous weapon in your possession.

Dangerous Weapons

Handguns are not the only dangerous weapons that violate the law.
A dangerous weapon is any firearm or object designed, made, or adopted for the purpose of inflicting death or serious physical injury.

Examples of dangerous weapons are:
- All firearms
- Knife with a blade of three (3) inches or longer
- Double-headed knife of any length
- Razor
- Switch blade knives
- Gravity knife
- Stiletto (any length)
- Ice pick
- Sword
- Dagger
- Billy club
- Bludgeon
- Brass knuckles
- Nunchaku (fighting sticks)
- Shuriken (throwing star)
- Any weapon or object intended to cause injury to another [3]

Busted

Again, why is there a need for an 18-year-old to possess a gun? Or, to attend a high school football game with a gun?

An 18-year-old has drawn a three-year prison sentence for being caught with a gun at the Texas High-Arkansas High football game in Texarkana. [1]

Busted

If you do own or possess illegal weapons, why would a person advertise that fact by posing on MySpace or Facebook with them?

A 16-year-old boy in Jefferson, Colorado, was arrested after police say he showed pictures of himself on his MySpace page holding handguns. Police subsequently found the same weapons in his home, says Jim Shires of the Jefferson County Sheriff's Office. The boy has been charged with three misdemeanors for being a juvenile in possession of handguns... [2]

Destructive Devices

It is illegal to possess or own destructive devices.

In some states, destructive weapons are considered different from deadly weapons. Illegal destructive devices can be:
- Explosives
- Incendiary or poison gas bombs
- Grenades
- Rockets
- Missiles
- Landmines
- Other similar items

Use of Mace

In most states, the use of mace is prohibited.

Spray Devices

Spray devices containing less than 35 grams are usually lawful if used for your protection or the protection of personal property and your use of physical force is justified. Please check your local regulations.

Lawful Force

You are permitted to use force to protect yourself, but it must be reasonable force under the circumstances.

Deadly Force

You can only use deadly force if you have a reasonable fear for your own life. [4]

Busted

Yet again, unthinking postings on social Internet sites lead to serious legal consequences.

When Judge Brian Boatright of Jefferson County, Colorado, found a 16-year-old Evergreen High School student standing before him guilty of a weapons charge last month, the strongest evidence hadn't come from a police search, a neighbor's tip, or even a wiretap.

The evidence had been supplied by the teen, who this year had posted pictures of himself surrounded by guns on his page of the social networking website MySpace.com.

MySpace and its cousins, Xanga and Facebook, have…attracted more than 100 million users, most of them young people creating their own pages to show off to friends. Law enforcement officials, however, have another use for them: They are fast becoming a crucial source of evidence in crimes involving young people ranging from pornography to drugs to terrorist threats.

Last month, Kansas police thwarted a plot for a Columbine-style shooting involving five boys, based on a MySpace posting citing the planned violence. It was at least the fourth Columbine-style plot this year revealed through MySpace or Xanga.

But the rapid increase in law enforcement use of MySpace, including security officers who routinely monitor the sites in high schools across the country, has caught the attention of civil libertarians and Internet advocates, who worry that in some cases students whose behavior would otherwise pass unnoticed are being subjected to extra scrutiny…

Longtime Internet researcher Dana Michele Boyd described information on the Web as "super public"—remaining available indefinitely, searchable at any time, and accessible by anyone.

While conversations in public spaces might be overheard by passersby, the potential pool of listeners is limited and the conversation itself is ephemeral, explain Boyd, who studies teens and social networking at the University of California, Berkeley.

But the very qualities of the Internet that make it a powerful and democratic communications tool—its openness and availability to everybody—put teens under a level of scrutiny normally devoted to paparazzi-hounded celebrities, Boyd said.

"We're looking at all this online stuff with a strictness we never did offline," she said. Most teenagers, she added, assume that their audience on the Web is their peers—and not parents, school officials, or the police. [5]

Busted

Student violence and possession of weapons also occurs outside of the United States.

Calls for tough action after a chilling increase in Scottish pupils excluded for carrying weapons.

Soaring numbers of armed thugs are being thrown out of Scotland's schools for attacking pupils and teachers.

The epidemic of violence sees almost two children excluded from school every day for using a weapon, a rise of 28 per cent.

A growing number of pupils are being sent home after being discovered with alcohol or drugs.

Parents will be alarmed to discover that Scotland's shameful blade culture is spreading from the streets to the classrooms.

It also piles more pressure on Education Secretary Fiona Hyslop only weeks after it emerged that teacher numbers have sunk to a three-year low. [8]

Gun Violence Stats

American children are more at risk from firearms than the children of any other industrialized nation. In one year, firearms killed no children in Japan, 18 in Great Britain, 57 in Germany, 109 in France, 153 in Canada, and 5,285 in the United States. [6]

Teen Gun Stats

- The latest National Teen Gun Survey (2009) revealed that more than one in four teens knows someone who has been shot—and more than one in three teens fear being shot one day.
- Twelve percent (12%) of teens say that at least one student from their school has been killed by gun violence in the past year.
- Nearly half of African American teens know someone who has been shot.
- Thirty-four percent (34%) of teens say they could get a handgun if they really wanted to.
- Eight in ten teens say they would inform an adult if someone they knew had an illegal gun.
- Sixty-nine percent (69%) of teens say adults are not doing enough to prevent gun violence. [7]

Chapter Five
SEXUAL ACTIVITY, CHILD PORNOGRAPHY, AND DATE RAPE

● ● ● ● ● ● ● ●

Sexual Activity

If you force or compel any person to engage in sexual activity or even sexual contact it is a crime. This is the case even if you have been dating each other or have known each other for a long time. It is illegal to engage in physical violence, threaten a person, or give a person drugs or alcohol to take advantage of the person. You have to carefully control your behavior in this area if you are 18 or older and have sex with someone under 16. Even with their consent you can be charged with a sex crime and/or child molestation. All it would take to face such charges would be a call to the police from one of the parents of your sex partner or another person aware of your conduct. Never assume that you are safe. Never engage in sex with an underage person or you could face dire consequences.

In addition, it is a crime if you are 19 or older to engage in a sexual act with any person under 16 who is five years or younger than you, even if the other person consents.

Is It Legal?

Is it legal for an 18-year-old boy to date a 15-year-old girl in the State of California? Yes, because there are no laws that restrict "dating." But an 18-year-old male cannot have lawful sex with a 15-year-old in any state in America. There are age of consent laws regarding the age at which a person can engage in consensual sex. In California, and in most states, that age is 18.

Some states make exceptions when both parties engaged in sexual intercourse are minors.[1]

Busted

Sex with an underage person can have severe consequences.

Ricky is a 19-year-old boy; he has asked that Fox 23 not disclose his last name in fear of vigilante's. Under the Oklahoma State Department of Corrections Sex and Violent Crime Offender Registry, Ricky is charged with Lewd or Indecent Proposals/Act To A Child.

At age 16, in Iowa, Ricky says he had sex with a girl who told him she was 16-years-old.

It was not until an officer showed up at his door telling him the girl was really 13-years-old that he knew her true age.

In a plea agreement, Ricky was sentenced to two years probation and ten years on the sex offender registry.

Since then an Iowa judge expunged Ricky's case but three years later he has moved to Oklahoma and says it has been nothing but a nightmare. Now he wants to warn other teens it could happen to them.

"I don't have anything but my mom or my little brother or my family and nothing else," says Ricky.

However, Ricky says he does have hope. Hope he can just be a teenager again.

Instead this 19-year-old boy is branded a child rapist for having sex with a teenage girlfriend who told him she was 16-years-old.

"It's a nightmare to wake up every day just hoping that something will change," says Ricky.

Ricky's mother, Mary Duval is legally blind so Ricky has to take care of his family but he cannot find a job.[2]

Busted

This is a tragic story involving consenting minors that has had devastating consequences on peoples' careers, future lives and family.

After a wild New Year's Eve party (January 1, 2005), six Douglasville teens found themselves charged with child molestation under a legal technicality. The boy who refused to take a plea now faces a decade behind bars.

Around 3 A.M., Michelle awoke from a drunken daze. She was lying on the floor between two double beds and wearing nothing but socks. In a panic, she called her mother from a cell phone, asking—no, pleading—for her to come now. Michelle managed to find her overnight bag and scrounged up a shirt and underwear to wear outside. Her mother picked her up in front of the hotel.

Once they got in the car, Michelle's mother told her daughter that she reeked of liquor and marijuana and as soon as they got home she needed to take a bath. Michelle got into the tub, but then broke down and told her upset mom, "I think they raped me." She dressed, and mother and daughter headed to the Douglasville Police Department. After they filed a report, investigators ordered Michelle to go to a hospital for an examination.

Later that morning, loud knocks at the doors of rooms 135 and 136 awakened the stragglers still there. Officers announced that they were there to investigate a gang rape that had been reported by Michelle. The youngsters sat around bleary-eyed as detectives questioned them; meantime, after securing a search warrant, officers scoured the rooms for evidence, carefully collecting almost a dozen used condoms and wrappers that were found strewn about the floor and in wastebaskets.

Just as they were wrapping up their search, detective Ed Reece, a crime scene technician, noticed something in the corner of the room: the video camera.

Over the next few days, investigators interviewed about 14 teens who had been at the party. Eventually five young men admitted to detectives that they had engaged in sexual intercourse with Michelle and that Tracy had performed oral sex on them. Officers continued tracking down evidence.

After the Christmas holiday break, on the first day of the second semester of his long-awaited senior year, Genarlow Wilson's charmed life came to a screeching halt. The football player and track star, homecoming king, and honor-roll student was met by sheriff's deputies in his Douglas County High classroom. Genarlow and his friend Narada Williams, who had also attended the now-notorious party, were marched in handcuffs through the same hallways that had been filled with happy memories. It all seemed surreal, but it didn't take long for Genarlow to realize that this was no dream.

Along with Genarlow and Narada, Ryan Barnwell, Cortez Robinson, Adrien Willis, and Frankie Henry—all 17 years old—were arrested on a host of charges including rape, contributing to the delinquency of a minor, aggravated sodomy, and aggravated child molestation.

As lawyers and detectives met with the boys and their families, the impact of the charges began to sink in. Clearly, rape is illegal in all American states, but in Georgia, sex, including oral sex, with anyone under the age of 16 can be classified as aggravated child molestation—even if it occurs between two teens less than three years apart in age, as in the instance of 17-year-old Genarlow and 15-year-old Tracy.

In fact, under Georgia law, the penalty is actually more severe for a person found guilty of engaging in oral sex with a minor than for having intercourse (which is classified as misdemeanor statutory rape), even if the perpetrator is just a few years older than the minor.

The trial began the morning of February 21, 2005, at the Douglas County Courthouse…Genarlow was scared, trembling at times, but he held on to the conviction that no fair-minded juror could look at that videotape, hear the testimony of others who attended that party, and, in good conscience, call him a child molester.

He would have seemed to be a model defendant. Attractive, popular, and outgoing, Genarlow had been headed for a bright future. He had a 3.2 grade point average and athletic abilities that kept college coaches calling to offer football and track scholarships. He was All Conference in football both his junior and senior years. He was voted 11th-grade prom prince and his senior year was capped off with a distinguished honor: He was elected Douglas County High's first-ever homecoming king.

Normally extroverted and upbeat, Genarlow was sedate and still as he listened to Michelle, the mothers of both girls, his friends, and friends of the alleged victims testify at the five-day trial that played out with the intensity of a television drama.

But the courtroom showdowns were no match for the fallout that followed the reading of the verdict. Genarlow's mother, who had been awaiting word from home, raced into the courtroom with her young daughter in tow just in time for the announcement. It was standing room only, with people even lining the walls, as jury forewoman Marie Manigault stood up in the jury stand and read, "We, the jury, find the defendant, Genarlow Raevion Wilson, not guilty of rape. We, the jury, find the defendant, Genarlow Raevion Wilson, guilty of aggravated child molestation this 25th day of February 2005."

The room erupted into a collective gasp and Genarlow, dressed in a plaid button-down and khakis, sunk his face into his hands and began sobbing uncontrollably. His mother clutched her young daughter and cried as two armed guards handcuffed her son and led him out of the courtroom.

The jury filed into the back room where they had deliberated for about five hours earlier that day. It was not until then, says Manigault, that attorney Michael Mann told them that their verdict meant a mandatory 10-year sentence for Genarlow. The room exploded. "People were screaming, crying, beating against the walls," she recalls. "I just went limp. They had to help me to a chair."

At the time that Genarlow's trial was underway, just down the hall in the same courthouse, Douglas County Judge Robert James Baker was hearing the case of Alexander High School English teacher and cheering coach Kari McCarley. The 27-year-old was found guilty of having a sexual relationship with a 17-year-old male student who attended the school where she worked. She was sentenced to three years probation and 90 days in jail.

"I just could not live with myself having that label [of child molester] for the rest of my life," Genarlow says, beaming at the sight of his mother. "Even after serving time in prison I would have to register as a sex offender wherever I lived and if I applied for a job for the rest of my life, all for participating in a consensual sex act with a girl just two years younger than me," he says, his voice trailing off. "It's a lifelong sentence in itself. I AM NOT A CHILD MOLESTER!" [3]

U.S. Teen Sexual Activity January 2005

General Sexual Activity

- Fewer than half of 9-12th grade students report having had sexual intercourse, reflecting a decline during the last decade from 53% in 1993 to 47% in 2003. Males are more likely than females to report having had sexual intercourse.

- The percentage of high school students who have had sexual intercourse increases by grade. In 2003, 62% of 12th graders had had sexual intercourse, compared with 33% of 9th graders.

First Sexual Intercourse

- The median age at first intercourse is 16.9 years for boys and 17.4 years for girls.

- The percentage of teens 15-19 who had initiated sexual intercourse before age 14 has decreased in recent years, from a high of 8% of girls and 11% of boys in 1995 to a low of 6% of girls and 8% of boys in 2002.

Sexual Partners and Relationships

- The percentage of 9-12th grade students who report having had four or more sexual partners has declined in recent years from 19% in 1993 to 14% in 2003. Males (18%) are

● ● ● ● ● ●

39

more likely than females (11%) to report having had four or more sexual partners.
* Most (74%) sexually active females aged 15-19 have partners who are the same age or 1-3 years older; for a quarter of girls, their first partners were 4 or more years older. The younger a girl is when she has sex for the first time, the greater the average age difference is likely to be between her and her partner.

Abstinence
* In 2003, 66% of high school students were currently abstinent, meaning they had not engaged in sexual intercourse over the last 3 months.
* Among teens aged 15-17 who have never had sexual intercourse. 94% said that concern about pregnancy influenced their decision to wait. Similar numbers said that concern about HIV/AIDS (92%), other STDs (92%), and feeling "too young" (91%) contributed to their choice.

Sexual Pressure, Assault, and Dating Violence
* One third (33%) of sexually active teens 15-17 reported "being in a relationship where they felt things were moving too fast sexually," and 24% had "done something sexual they didn't really want to do." More than one in five (21%) reported having oral sex to "avoid having sexual intercourse" with a partner.
* More than a quarter (29%) of teens 15-17 report feeling pressure to have sex.
* Nearly one in 10 (9%) 9-12th grade students report having been physically forced to have sexual intercourse when they did not want to at some point. Females (12%) were more likely than males (6%) to report this experience. [4]

Child Pornography

You should be keenly aware that it is illegal to download certain material onto your computer:

* It is illegal to possess child pornography.
* It is illegal to download and keep sexual pictures of children and young teens.
* It is a crime to have child pornography (any material depicting a person under 18 performing or simulating sexual conduct).

The FBI and other federal agencies have placed high priority on enforcing federal statutes against the possession, distribution, and production of child pornography.

Busted

Matters that you may think of as being funny at the time can result in felonies and negatively impact the rest of your life.

Committing a felony is easier than most teens—and their parents—might realize.

All a teen needs is his or her computer and a cell phone camera to commit crimes that carry a maximum sentence of 7 years in prison and a $15,000 fine, according to Jeff Conrad, a former assistant district attorney who has prosecuted people accused of sex crimes.

Conrad outlined a hypothetical scenario for the commission of a serious crime at a meeting on Internet safety recently held for the parents of students in Hempfield School District.

"Your kids go to a party," he said. "Someone has a cell phone (camera), and one of their buddies happens to get all buck naked. They go home and think it's funny. So they put it on the Internet and sent it out to their buddies."

When the person takes a photo of a naked minor, he's committing a felony of the third degree. Though the teen probably doesn't think of it this way, the photographer has just created child pornography.

When he puts it on the Internet and sends it out to his buddies, he commits another felony, dissemination of child pornography. Each of his buddies who pass it on also can be charged with dissemination of child pornography.

Anyone who saves that picture on his computer can be charged with possession of child pornography, another felony, Conrad said…

For example, a boyfriend and girlfriend who videotape themselves having sex with each other might think it's "cute and endearing" for themselves to watch, said Assistant District Attorney, Rebecca Franz, who prosecutes juvenile sex offenders said. However, they aren't considering the ramifications of that video going online.

Assistant District Attorney Todd Kriner is working on a case in which a video shot by a couple was stolen from the boyfriend's house. Kriner said it was disseminated everywhere: "on the Internet, at school, at parties, everything." When the girlfriend's father found out about it, he called the police.

The case put the district attorney's office in the position of prosecuting teenagers for third-degree felonies: It is a felony to take pictures of someone under 18 engaging in any kind of sex act or nudity that is "depicted for such purpose of sexual stimulation or gratification of any person who might use such depiction," according to state law.

It is also a felony to disseminate those pictures by sending them over a cell phone, posting them on an Internet site like MySpace or Facebook, e-mailing them, or printing them and showing them around. It is also a felony to possess child pornography, like storing it on your computer.

Franz is prosecuting a case in which a teen is accused of possessing child pornography. She said the teen went on the Internet and downloaded photos and videos of child pornography.

"Kids have a false sense of security with computers, you know," Franz said. They may think that they can hide things, that no one can access their computer, that putting indecent pictures of themselves on MySpace is just funny.

Kids need to know that the district attorney's office can locate any information that is sent through electronic media, whether it's deleted or not, said Karen Mansfield, an assistant district attorney.

Even if teens are not caught and prosecuted, the attorneys said, the consequences still can be lifelong.

"They don't realize," Kriner said, "that once it's on the Internet, it's everywhere, for everybody, and somebody who wants it can get it and pretty much do whatever they want to with it, whether it's a picture or a movie."

If teens knew the pictures they took for fun may be downloaded and used for some child predator's sexual gratification, they might realize it's not a good idea, Franz said.

Also, those pictures could haunt them in the future.

"Once it's on the computer, it's there for the rest of your life," Mansfield said. "So, if you're 16 and doing something with your boyfriend or taking pictures, when you're 80 you probably can still see that picture."

Employers, colleges, and military recruiters are checking applicants' trails on the Internet and finding those pictures, Conrad warned parents. [5]

Do not post nude pictures of yourself or friends who are under 18 on the Internet.

Sexual Activity, Child Pornography, and Date Rape

Busted

Here is a real-life example of the above warning. Although taking place in Canada, the same result could occur in the United States.

It is one thing to have naked pictures of your underage girlfriend on your cell phone.

It's quite another to show them to your friends and e-mail them around.

That's where it can cross the line from innocent consensual sex games to child pornography charges and the possibility of a mandatory jail term.

A good example is a current case in northern Alberta, where an 18-year-old man is charged with possession of child pornography and distribution of child pornography.

The allegations are that a 17-year-old girl took a series of nude photographs of herself and e-mailed them to the man's cell phone. He later showed them to others.

Sources say the girl's father got wind of what happened and went storming to the local detachment and the resulting investigation led to an arrest and charges.

Legal experts say there is nothing criminal about two people in a consensual relationship sharing X-rated photos, even if one of them is under 18, as long as the older person is relatively close in age and not in a position of trust.

But, as soon as you start sharing the pictures with others, you have technically become a child porn distributor. [6]

Busted

Think before you send nude photos electronically to anyone.

Last month, three girls (ages 14 or 15) in Greensburg, Pennsylvania, were charged with disseminating child pornography for sexting their boyfriends. The boys who received the images were charged with possession. A teenager in Indiana faces felony obscenity charges for sending a picture of his genitals to female classmates. A 15-year-old girl in Ohio and a 14-year-old girl in Michigan were charged with felonies for sending nude images of themselves to classmates. Some of these teens have pleaded guilty to lesser charges. Others have not. If convicted, these young people may have to register as sex offenders, in some cases for a decade or two. Similar charges have been brought in cases reported in Alabama, Connecticut, Florida, New Jersey, New York, Pennsylvania, Texas, Utah, and Wisconsin. [9]

It's the Law: Montana

Bozeman, Montana, has a law that bans all sexual activity between members of the opposite sex in the front yard of a home after sundown—if they're nude. [7]

It's the Law: Virginia

In Romboch, Virginia, it is illegal to engage in sexual activity with the lights on. [8]

Busted

To further emphasize this point, here is still another example of the risks associated with distributing sexually explicit pictures:

"You go online to gloat to your friends about the stupid things you've done—or to embarrass the heck out of them," longtime Internet researcher, Danah Michele Boyd, said. "The number of teens who worry about their image with adults is very small."

That nonchalance is landing teens across the country in legal trouble. Seventeen-year-old Ryan Zylstra of Michigan is facing three counts relating to child pornography and up to 20 years in prison based on a prank gone wrong.

He allegedly posted a photo of two friends having sex—a 16-year-old girl and a 17-year-old boy—on his Xanga page, distributing sexually explicit images of minors under 18 is illegal under Michigan's child pornography laws.

The prosecutor has offered Zylstra a chance to plead guilty to one of the charges, which carries a possible seven-year term; he has so far rejected the deal, his lawyer said.

Zylstra is not the only teen facing prison time for material posted on the Internet. Three people in Rhode Island, two 16-year-old girls and one 19-year-old woman, face child pornography charges for allegedly posting sexually explicit pictures of themselves on MySpace.

Many youths don't try to cover their tracks online, but when they do their efforts often fail.

"They are stupidly believing that they're somehow anonymous because they created a fake Yahoo address when they post on MySpace," said Parry Aftab, a New Jersey lawyer and Internet specialist.

MySpace often aids in investigations to uncover posters' real identities. Though the company's official stance is that it is not an arm of law enforcement, it takes allegations of crime on the site seriously.[10]

Sexting

More teens caught up in sexting. Many don't realize porn charges can be attached.

A growing number of teens are ending up in serious trouble for sending racy photos with their cell phones.

Police have investigated more than two dozen teens in at least six states this year for sending nude images of themselves in cell phone text messages, which can bring a charge of distributing child pornography. Authorities typically are notified by parents or schools about so-called "sexting."

This week in Spotsylvania, VA, two boys, ages 15 and 18, were charged with solicitation and possession of child porn with intent to distribute after an investigation found they sought nude pictures from three juveniles—one in elementary school.

"It's absolutely becoming a bigger problem," says Michelle Collins of the National Center for Missing & Exploited Children.

Of the 2,100 children the center has identified as victims of online porn, she says, one-fourth initially sent the images themselves.

She says some did it for fun and others were tricked into it by adults they met online.

"They may not realize the danger they are exposing themselves to," says William Shaw, district attorney for Clearfield County, PA. "When they put it online, they lose control."

Last month, Shaw filed a juvenile petition against a 15-year-old girl for sending nude photos of herself over the Internet. He says his objective isn't to jail her but to get her counseling or other help. The 27-year-old man who enticed her to do it has been sentenced to 10 years for having sex with her.

Lawmakers are debating penalties. On Wednesday, the Utah legislature reduced penalties, from a felony to a misdemeanor, for sexting.

In Cuyahoga County, Ohio, Juvenile Court Judge Thomas O'Malley struggled to figure out what to do with eight teens, 14 to 17, caught trading nude cell phone pictures of themselves. He says the father of one of the girls found the images.

If the 17-year-old who sent the nude photos to an ex-boyfriend were convicted of a child porn charge, he says, she would be a registered sex offender for 20 years.

"These kids have no record, not even a parking ticket," says O'Malley, a father of four teens.

He required each to do community service and to ask peers if they knew sexting was a crime. They told O'Malley they surveyed 225 teens: 31 knew.[11]

Date Rape

> Date rape is "non-consensual sexual activity between people who are already acquainted, or know each other socially—friends, acquaintances, people on a date, or even people in an existing relationship—where it is alleged that consent for sexual activity was not given, or was given under duress."[12]

Date rape is also referred to as contact rape, acquaintance rape, and sleep rape.

Date Rape Rate
Do Not Think This Cannot Happen to You

Astoundingly, date rape is "committed at a shocking rate of once every two minutes in North America."[13]

As reprehensible as this horrible conduct is, it is astounding how often this offense occurs.

Date Rape Drugs

Date rape drugs include:
- GBH (Gauma Hydroxybutyric Acid)
- Rohypol (Flunitrazepm or "Roofies")
- Ketamine (Ketamine Hydrochloride)
- Benzodiazepines (such as flunitrazepam)

To protect yourself from being a victim of date rape:
- Do not accept drinks from other people, except trusted friends.
- Always open containers yourself.
- Keep your drink with you at all times, even when you go to the bathroom.
- Do not share drinks.
- Do not drink from a punch bowl or large, common, or open container. They may already have drugs in them.
- Do not drink anything that tastes or smells strange. Sometimes GBH tastes salty.
- Have a non-drinking friend with you to make sure nothing happens.[14]

Date rape drugs may be slipped into your drink while you are not suspecting it. The effect of the drugs can make you helpless, making it easy for you to become the victim of a sexual assault.

The drugs are usually odorless and tasteless and you may not be able to recall what happened.

Sexual Assault: What Is It?

For sexual activity to be all right, it must be consensual, which means that both people want it to happen. Sexual assault is when any person forces you to participate in a sexual act when you do not want to. This can include touching or penetrating the vagina, mouth, or anus of the victim (often called rape); touching the penis of the victim; or forcing the victim to touch the attacker's vagina, penis, or anus. Touching can mean with a hand, finger, mouth, penis, or just about anything else, including objects.

Sexual Assault: Intimidation

It does not always take physical force to sexually assault a victim. Attackers can use threats or intimidation to make a victim feel afraid or unable to refuse them. It is also sexual assault if the victim is drunk, drugged, unconscious, too young (ages of consent differ from state to state), or mentally disabled to be legally able to agree to sexual contact. [15]

Sexual Assault: By Someone You Know

Most victims are assaulted by someone they know: a friend, date, acquaintance, or boyfriend or girlfriend. Dating or being sexually involved with someone does not give that person the right to force you to have sexual contact you do not want. Even if you have had sex before, you have the right to say "NO" at any time. You are also allowed to change your mind at any time. Being sexually assaulted is never your fault.

Say "No" Assertively

You must be assertive and say "no" when you mean no. Assertiveness is different from rudeness (which is aggressive). Being assertive simply means saying directly and clearly what you mean. A simple "no" can resolve most unwanted touches. You could say:
- "Stop, please. I am not enjoying this."
- "Get your hands off me."
- "I do not want to have sex."
- "I said 'no' and I mean no." [16]

Rape Stats

- A woman is sexually assaulted every 2 minutes in America.
- 86% or rapes are committed by someone the survivor knows.
- 38% of date rape survivors are females between the ages of 14 to 17.
- 42.5% of assaults happen in the victim's own home.
- 78% of teens do not tell their parents that they have been raped.
- 71% of rape survivors tell a friend.
- Only 3% of rapes result in pregnancy. [17]

If You are a Victim of Sexual Assault, You Might:

- Feel afraid, ashamed, angry, sad, lonely, betrayed or depressed
- Feel guilty and confused if you know or had a relationship with the attacker, even though the assault was not your fault.
- Feel like you have no friends or that your friends will not believe you
- Want to hurt someone else or yourself
- Feel like taking steps to defend yourself
- Feel helpless to stop the assault
- Feel helpless about whether anything can be done
- Be afraid to go anywhere that the attacker might be
- Feel anxious all the time
- Feel bad about yourself or your body [18]

Sexual Assault Stats

- Sexual assault is a widespread and underreported crime.
- In 2005, law enforcement in the United States received 69,370 reports of rapes.
- In 2005, more than 170,000 women and 15,000 men were victims of attempted or completed rapes.
- More teens are raped by people they know than they are by strangers. [19]

Teen Stats

During the past year, 9.2% of students nationwide had been hit, slapped, or physically hurt on purpose by their boyfriend or girlfriend (dating violence). [20]

Rape Stats

In a Rhode Island study with high school students, over 50% of males and 42% of females agreed that there were times when it was "acceptable for a male to hold a female down and physically force her to engage in intercourse."

Seventy-five (75%) percent of women raped are between the ages of 15 and 21. The average age is 18.

About 75% of the men and at least 55% of the women involved in acquaintance rapes had been drinking or taking drugs just before the attack.

Sixty-two percent (62%) of completed rapes occur by classmates or friends.

Fifty-seven percent (57%) of rapes occur while out on a date. [21]

Teen Rape Stats

Teens 16 to 19 were three and one-half times more likely than the general population to be victims of rape, attempted rape, or sexual assault. [22]

Teen Date Rape Do's and Don'ts: Tips on Avoiding Date Rape

Rape is not always avoidable, but there are some things you can do to reduce the risk of being a date rape victim:

Don'ts

- Avoid parties or groups where alcohol and/or drug use is excessive. Studies of date rape show that 75% of the date-rapists and 55% of the victims had been drinking or taking drugs before the rape occurred.
- Do not drink or use drugs and do not get in a car with someone you don't know well.
- Avoid people who make you feel uncomfortable.
- Never walk home through deserted areas like parkland or railroad tracks.

- Do not hitchhike.
- Try not to do things alone.
- When you are leaving, do not announce that you are walking alone. Try to walk home with a friend or in groups.
- Do not give a bunch of information about yourself to a person you just met. [23]

Do's

- Stay in control.
- If you are going to a party, establish a buddy system with a friend and watch out for each other. Also, consider sticking to group dates.
- Always carry a cell phone or phone card and some extra money for a taxi in case you need to get out of a bad situation or just want to go home.
- Learn how to defend yourself.
- Decide what your limits are and remember that a person who pressures you to change your standards does not care about you and should be avoided.
- People cannot read your mind. If someone is trying to force you into doing something you do not want, loudly tell him or her "no" and get away. Making noise can attract help and scare your attacker.
- Trust your instincts. If you do not feel comfortable with a person or situation, get away. [23]

Genarlow Wilson: Update
(please see pages 38 & 39)

A Georgia judge called Genarlow Wilson's 10-year sentence for consensual teen sex "a grave miscarriage of justice" and ordered him released from prison. But the former high school football star and scholar remains behind bars pending a notice of appeal.

Wilson's sentence—along with the explicit details of his case—continues to stir national debate with supporters, including former President Jimmy Carter, who say his sentence was too severe.

In July 2003, a videotape surfaced showing Wilson, then 17, engaging in consensual oral sex with a 15-year-old girl at a hotel party hosted by fellow high-schoolers. A jury later found Wilson guilty of aggravated child molestation, which carries a mandatory 10-year sentence and requires placement on Georgia's sex offender registry.

An interesting exception in Georgia law would have given Wilson just one year in prison if he and the girl had engaged in sexual intercourse. Since Wilson's conviction, that loophole has been closed by state lawmakers.

If upheld, Monday's ruling by the judge will void Wilson's 10-year sentence and reclassify it as a misdemeanor with a 12-month term. The 21-year-old will get credit for time served and will not be required to register as a sex offender.

Judge Thomas H. Wilson said, "The fact that Genarlow Wilson has spent two years in prison for what is now classified as a misdemeanor, and without assistance from this court will spend eight more years in prison, is a grave miscarriage of justice." The judge is not related to Genarlow Wilson.

But Attorney General Thurbert Baker disagrees. He is challenging the judge's authority to commute the sentence and is taking his appeal to the Georgia Supreme Court.

Wilson also was charged with rape, along with five other males who accepted plea deals, for having sex with another 17-year-old girl at the party. He was acquitted of that charge. [24]

● ● ● ● ● ● ● ●

47

Early Warning Signs That Your Date May Eventually Become Abusive

- Extreme jealousy
- Controlling behavior
- Quick involvement
- Unpredictable mood swings
- Alcohol and drug use
- Explosive anger
- Isolates you from friends/family
- Uses force during an argument
- Shows hypersensitivity
- Believes in rigid sex roles
- Blames others for problems/feelings
- Cruel to animals/children
- Verbally abusive
- Abused former partners
- Threatens violence[25]

Common Clues that Indicate a Teenager May be Experiencing Dating Violence

- Physical signs of injury
- Use of drugs/alcohol
- Truancy, dropping out of school
- Pregnancy
- Failing grades
- Emotional outburst
- Indecision
- Isolation[27]
- Changes in mood or personality

More Dating Safety Tips

- Consider double-dating the first few times you go out with a new person.
- Before leaving on a date, know the exact plans for the evening and make sure a parent or friend knows these plans and what time to expect you home. Let your date know that you are expected to call or tell that person when you get in.
- Be aware of your decreased ability to react under the influence of alcohol or drugs.
- If you leave a party with someone you do not know well, make sure you tell another person you are leaving and with whom. Ask a friend to call and make sure you arrived home safely.
- Assert yourself when necessary. Be firm and straightforward in your relationships. [26]

Violence: 30%-50%

- In one study, from 30 to 50 percent of female high school students reported having already experienced teen dating violence.
- Teen dating violence most often takes place in the home of one of the partners.[28]

Teen Dating Stats

- A survey of adolescent and college students revealed that date rape accounted for 67 percent of sexual assaults.[29]

Violence: 1 in 5

- One in five—20 percent of dating couples—report some type of violence in their relationships.
- One of five college females will experience some form of dating violence.
- A survey of 55 young women, ages 15 to 24, found that 60 percent were currently involved in an ongoing abusive relationship and all participants had experienced violence in a dating relationship.
- Six out of 10 rapes of young women occur in their own home or a friend or relative's home, not in a dark alley.[30]

Teen Dating Stats

Sixty percent (60%) of college-aged males reported that they would use force in their sexual relations with women if they were sure they would not get caught.

This is an awful statistic...Some studies suggest that up to one in every four women are victimized by some form of sexual assault in their lifetimes.[31]

Chapter Six
STALKING, CYBERSTALKING, AND CYBERBULLYING

● ● ● ● ● ● ● ●

Stalking

It is natural to be emotionally upset if you break up with your partner, but this does not enable you to stalk, threaten, or harass that person. As an adult, you are expected by the laws of society to control your emotions and act responsibly. Perhaps owing to many instances of celebrity cases, the offense of stalking has been enforced more frequently today and enhanced protective laws have been passed in most states.

Stalking is defined by the law as "the willful, malicious, and repeated following or harassing of another person."

You are entitled by the law not to be harassed, threatened, stalked, or a victim of violence.

Protective Order

You can obtain a protective order from a court if you and the person threatening your safety have lived together or are or were sexual partners. A protective order is delivered to the person you are seeking protection from and to the local police.

If you did not live together, you can secure a protective order from harassment (this includes stalking).

The protective order can afford you immediate temporary relief. Depending on the state you live in, after a court hearing, the protection can be extended up to two years, and is generally renewable on request. Persons who violate protective orders can be placed in jail for up to one year.

There are also protections from criminal law that a person can use in conjunction with the police. Jail time can result from violations of these laws. [1]

Anti-Stalking Laws

Some state anti-stalking laws require that there be both:
- A "credible threat;" and
- The appearance that the perpetrator intends, and has the ability, to carry out that threat.

Credible Threat

A credible threat is a verbal or written threat of violence made against a person by a perpetrator.

Stalking Categories

Stalking:
- Is a misdemeanor in some states
- In other states, the first offense is a misdemeanor and subsequent offenses are felonies
- Other states make it a felony[2]

Stalking Stats

A survey by the United States Justice Department has found that stalking is affecting 3.4 million Americans every year with tens of thousand losing their jobs, fleeing their homes, or fearing for their safety as a result of the stalking.

Over 10% of victims said they have suffered for five or more years and one in seven said stalking had forced them out of their homes. Women are twice as likely to be victims of stalkers than men.

More than one-third of the victims reported being followed or spied upon. Some said they were tracked by electronic monitoring, listening devices, or video cameras. About 21 percent said they had been attacked by their stalker—with the forms of assault ranging from a slap to rape.

…nearly 75% of victims tend to know their stalker, most commonly a former spouse or ex-boyfriend/girlfriend, sometime a relative or co-worker. [3]

Busted

E-mails and instant messages make communicating easier, but they also can breed a new kind of criminal: the Internet stalker.

While Illinois' cyberstalking law—passed in 2001—gives electronic harassment the same penalties as stalking in person, some say the problem is still budding.

Just last Saturday Tonny Home, of South Bend, Indiana, was indicted on charges of cyberstalking and criminal trespass for harassing Tamrom Hall, a news anchor for Chicago Fox affiliate WFLD, with repeated e-mails, letters and phone calls, said Tom Stanton, spokesman for the Cook County State's Attorney's office.

"They were mostly obscene in nature," Stanton said.

That is a classic example of what has led 42 states to write cyberstalking laws, said Jane Hitchcock, president of Working to Halt Online Abuse, an advocacy and support group for victims. In Illinois, web stalking is a felony punishable by up to three years in prison.

The state's first conviction for web harassment came this spring, Hitchcock said. Porfirios Liapis, of St. Charles, was sentenced on May 23 to 60 days in the Lake County Jail, 75 hours of public service, and $2,022 in fines and fees for e-mailing death threats to a friend, according to the Lake County Circuit Clerk's office.

In a separate case, Amy Defay, 23, of Rockford, was charged last month with cyberstalking for threatening a man. Defay sent at least two threatening e-mails that left the man's family with "reasonable apprehension for fear of bodily harm," said James Brun, Winnebago County Assistant State's Attorney.[4]

Variations In The Law

You have to review the law in your state:
- Some states define stalking to include threats made to the victims' immediate family
- Some states will deny bail for stalking
- Some states require counseling for the offender at the offender's expense
- Some states allow warrantless arrests of stalkers
- Some states consider stalking convictions in other states as previous violations and allow for enhanced penalties even if not committed in the same state

Regardless of the state you live in, never engage in this type of behavior, and if you are of the belief you are being stalked, report it immediately to the authorities.[5]

Busted

Breaking up with a girlfriend can be a very upsetting experience. You should not compound your emotions by engaging in stalking.

A Steuben, ME, teenage has been charged with stalking, terrorizing, and criminal trespass.

Kirk R. Potter, 18, appeared on Tuesday in Machias District Court, Maine, on the charges, all misdemeanors.

According to an arrest affidavit by Sgt. Dennis Perry of the Washington County Sheriff's Department, Potter had recently separated with a young female on Jan. 9.

Throughout the remainder of that week and into the weekend, the young man showed up at the girl's residence refusing to leave and called her cell phone repeatedly, Perry wrote. He was warned by police on one occasion not to return to her residence in Harrington.

Potter also reportedly followed the girl outside a chem-free dance on Jan. 11, grabbed her shoulders and pushed her up against a car, according to the document. The girl's parents came to pick her up but Potter kept calling her cell phone until nearly 3 a.m., the affidavit stated.

When Potter was finally arrested on Jan. 13, he had been following the alleged victim's car around...He reportedly threatened the girl and another male she was with during a telephone conversation, according to Perry.[6]

Stalking Stats

According to the Stalking Resource Center:
- 1,006,970 women and 370,990 men are stalked annually in the United States.
- 1 in 12 women and 1 in 45 men will be stalked in their lifetime.
- 77% of female and 64% of male victims know their stalker.
- 87% of stalkers are men.
- 59% of female victims and 30% of male victims are stalked by an intimate partner.
- 81% of women stalked by a current or former intimate partner are also physically assaulted by that partner.
- 31% of women stalked by a current or former intimate partner are also sexually assaulted by that partner.
- The average duration of stalking is 1.8 years.
- If stalking involves intimate partners, the average duration of stalking increases to 2.2 years.
- 61% of stalkers made unwanted phone calls, 33% sent or left unwanted letters or items, 29% vandalized property, and 9% killed or threatened to kill a family pet.
- 28% of female victims and 20% of male victims obtained a protective order. 69% of female victims and 81% of male victims had the protection order violated.[7]

Stalking on Campus Stats

In a study carried out from February to May 1997 involving 4,446 college women:
- 13% of college women were stalked during one, six to nine month period.
- 80% of campus stalking victims knew their stalkers.
- 3 in 10 college women reported being injured emotionally or psychologically from being stalked. [8]

Cyberstalking Consequences

Individuals have been cyberstalked for the most minor reasons by people they have angered in the past. Victims were targeted because they dumped a guy after less than a month, fired an employee, were part of a business deal gone badly, or—no joke—parked in the wrong parking spot.

One…well-off white male—a senior vice president of a well-known tax firm (was cyberstalked by) a fired employee (who) began sending hundreds of e-mails with Photoshopped pornographic images of the VP to every single person throughout the company for months before it was stopped. The executive was so humiliated he not only left his job, he left his life—changing his name and moving to a different state. The ease of causing someone trouble through technology, without having to leave the house, makes cyberstalkers out of people who would have normally fumed in silence. [9]

Cyberbullying

Cyberbullying is the harassment or tormenting of another person online. Below are some other common forms of cyberbullying:

Flaming

Flaming is the posting of derogatory remarks on someone else's webpage or instant messaging (IM) nasty remarks to someone. Mostly, it is online fights filled with bad language. One way to deal with flaming is to ignore it. Take down the post or block the person on IM. If you fight back, you are engaging in a flaming war and are just as culpable as the person who flamed you. Flaming wars can escalate into physical fights, which nobody wants. Of course you should call the local police if you believe you are in any danger.

Impersonation

Impersonation is when a person logs on to someone else's account and sends out messages pretending to be that user... This is a form of identity theft and it is a federal crime. Generally it is prosecuted as a Class C Felony, which can bring with it two to eight years in jail and up to $10,000 in fines depending on the harm inflicted by assuming another person's identity.

Denigration

Types of online denigration can include creating profiles that make fun of another person, erecting blogs that rate people in your class, or creating home pages that make fun of others. This can be taken very seriously by authorities. In her book *Totally Wired: What Teens and Tweens are Really Doing Online*, author Anastasia Goodstein tells the story of one Michigan parent whose daughter was expelled from school when she created a MySpace page that denigrated her home economics teacher.

Harassment And Cyberstalking

Harassment is the repetitive sending of offensive, rude, or insulting comments to an individual online. This behavior can escalate to stalking when the messages become threatening or intimidating to the point that the recipient becomes afraid for his/her own safety. Cyberstalking in most states is prosecuted under stalking laws.

Victims

If you are a victim of cyberbullying you have a variety of options. Below are some tips compiled from The Stalking Resource Center on what you should do if you are being bullied:

1. Ignore all messages. When someone harasses you by sending repeated messages and you respond to one of them...that tells them that they can get a response from you by bombarding you with messages. Report the messages to authorities if you sense any danger.
2. Block the harasser. But this will not always work.
3. Delete the profile, blog, e-mail, or IM account that is being attacked. If they do not know where to find you, they may not harass you. You can always start a new blog, profile, e-mail, or IM account.
4. Document the harassment. All text, IMs, and e-mails should be saved to show to the proper authorities if the harassment continues.
5. Trace anonymous messages. If you are getting e-mails from an anonymous source, it is possible to trace the IP address to a specific computer server. Online stalkers can be reported to your Internet service provider.
6. Call someone for help. Victim advocate associations like the Stalking Resource Center (800-FYI-CALL) or Safe Horizon can help you assess threats and explain your legal options.

Authorities take cyberbullying very seriously. So, before you respond with an angry e-mail or post a cruel comment on another person's profile or blog, stop and think first. You may save yourself from a lot of legal and disciplinary problems down the road. [10]

Teens Online Stats

- 71% of all teens have received online messages from someone they do not know.
- 45% have been asked for personal information by people they do not know.
- 61% have posted a personal profile on social networking websites such as MySpace, Friendster, or Xanga and half of them have posted pictures of themselves.
- 34% saw sexual material online that they did not want to see.
- 13% received online sexual solicitations.
- 9% were harassed in other ways. [11]

What Teens Think and Do Stats

- 40% think it is safe to respond to or chat with people they do not know.
- 20% think it is safe to share personal information on a public social networking website.
- 30% have considered meeting someone they have met online.
- 9% of 13-15 year-olds have actually met face-to-face with someone they first met online [12]

Cyberstalking Laws

An anti-stalking bill passed by Congress makes it a federal crime to "annoy" someone over the Internet. It is a federal crime, punishable by up to five years in prison and a fine of up to $250,000, to transmit any communication in interstate or foreign commerce containing a threat to injure the person of another.

Busted

Stalking, unfortunately, has become fairly common and anyone is likely to be a stalker.

A Cobb middle school teacher resigned Friday following his arrest for stalking a former student.

Joseph Placania, an eighth-grade science teacher at Durham Middle School, was arrested Thursday at the Crimes Against Children Unit, said Sgt. Dana Pierce, a Cobb police spokesman.

Placania, 40, allegedly began an affair with his former student, who is now 17-years-old, in May of 2007, Pierce said.

She broke off the relationship with him in April.

Placania claimed the two had a sexual affair, according to his arrest warrant.

Pierce said there is no evidence the relationship was sexual. But Placania took the girl to Tennessee at least once, Pierce said.

After she broke off the relationship with him, Placania continued to try to contact her at work, through text messages, and on her MySpace page, he said.

According to Placania's arrest warrant, he was seen outside Gold's Gym on Cobb Parkway in Kennesaw on April 30.

The warrant says: "It had been made clear to him that she did not want to be with him anymore; Mr. Placania also sent numerous e-mails and text messages that were unwanted after their relationship was over."

Placania was arrested and charged with one count of misdemeanor stalking. He was released on $5,000 bond from the Cobb County jail.

Jay Dillon, a school district spokesman, said Placania resigned Friday. Cobb County police notified the district of the arrest on Thursday, he said.

"He acknowledged what he had been charged with and offered his resignation," Dillon said.[13]

Cyberstalking Stats

Now several news organizations are reporting on a teen epidemic of Tech Stalking, a new twist to date abuse that includes cyberstalking and the use of text-messaging and cell phone calling to dominate, humiliate, and/or harass the young and impressionable, in most cases, teen girls.

"Alarming numbers of teens in dating relationships are being controlled, abused and threatened using simple tech devices," according to Teenage Research Unlimited, which conducted the nationwide survey of 615 teens 13 to 18.

- 30% said they have been text messaged or e-mailed 10, 20, or 30 times an hour by a partner wanting to check up on them.
- 18% said their partner used a social-networking site to harass them.
- 17% said their partner made them "afraid not to respond to a cell phone call, e-mail, IM, or text message."
- 10 % said they had been threatened in calls or messages.
- 58% of parents whose teens were physically assaulted by their partner did not know it had happened. [14]

Chapter Seven
HATE CRIMES

● ● ● ● ● ● ● ●

57

Hate Crimes

Hate Crimes

Hate crimes is an important area of the law that is getting increased attention and enhanced penalties. There is no place in a civilized society for people to be beaten, harassed, or threatened because of their sexual preferences; crosses burned on lawns of homes because of religious beliefs; or nooses hung in trees or in rear-windows of pick-up trucks at or near civil rights demonstrations.

Hate crimes are crimes committed because of the victim's race, gender, national origin, religion, sexual orientation, or other protected status. The federal government, most states, and many localities have enacted laws or regulations to define such acts as separate crimes in themselves or to augment penalties for existing crimes when motivated by hatred or bias. Because definitions vary across jurisdictions, acts such as lynching, assault while calling the victim derogatory names, cross burning, or making intimidating threats on the basis of the victim's race or other protected status might be considered hate crimes. Whatever the definition, statistics show that incidences of hate crime were on the rise in the late twentieth century.

During the last two decades, nearly every state has enacted a hate crime law of some kind or adopted sentence enhancements for existing crimes.[1]

Punishment

If you are found guilty of a hate crime, you can be fined or jailed and/or ordered to pay restitution for any actual damages or losses that are incurred (including medical bills).

Hate Crimes Stats

Hate crimes in the U.S. rose 7.8% in 2006, with racially motivated attacks accounting for more than half of 7,722 reported incidents. Religious bias represented one-fifth of hate crimes, and cases of sexual orientation discrimination nearly 16%.[3]

Busted

The law is taking incidents of hate crimes more and more seriously.

Police in Louisiana say they've arrested an 18-year-old accused of driving with two hangman's nooses dangling from his pickup truck.

The arrest came after the teen allegedly drove past a crowd of people who had attended a civil rights march earlier in the day. Thousands of demonstrators had been protesting about an hour away in Jena, Louisiana, in the wake of a 2006 incident that began with nooses being hung from a tree.

Police in Alexandria, Louisiana, say they've charged the teen (Jeremiah Musen) with charges that include inciting a riot and first-offense drunken driving.[2]

Busted

Teens are very prone to unintentionally commit hate crimes.

An Oviedo teenager was arrested Saturday after police said he hung a noose in his African American neighbor's tree, Oviedo Police Department Lt. Dennis Lynch said.

Andrew Mathews, 15, has been charged with simple assault and trespassing. Police are classifying the act as a hate crime, which enhances the severity of the offenses.[5]

Hate Crimes: Stiffer Sentences

The United States Supreme Court gave its approval on June 12, 1993, to a new approach to punishing hate crimes, ruling unanimously that states may impose harsher sentences on criminals who choose their victims on the basis of race, religion, or other personal characteristics.[6]

Busted

Gay bashing is a serious hate crime.

According to CNN, Southlake resident and Georgetown student Phillip Cooney, 19, was arrested Thursday for beating up a gay Georgetown student. Police have been looking for the person who attacked the man since September 9 and are calling the attack a hate crime because the suspect yelled anti-gay slurs during the attack, according to reports.

The injured student did a lot of the investigating on his own.

A friend of the injured student told him he overheard someone talking about the attack in a class, and wrote down the initials embroidered on that student's backpack.

The injured man went to the social networking site Facebook, and looked up all the people that matched initials until he came across and recognized Cooney, who he now says attacked him.[4]

Busted

Hate crimes are resulting in much stiffer punishment for violators, not only in the United States.

The fatal gay bashing of a Vancouver man in Stanley Park was a hate crime, reminiscent of Nazi Youth attacks in pre-war Germany, a Youth-Court judge declared yesterday.

As a result, in a rare judicial move, Judge Valmond Romilly went beyond a prosecutor's recommendation and imposed the maximum sentence—three years—on an underage teenager for his role in the death of Aaron Webster, killed by a gang of youths wielding golf clubs and baseball bats.

"It's entertainment," he told police who asked why the teenagers often headed to Stanley Park late a night to beat up people they called "peeping toms." He pleaded guilty to manslaughter in July.

Mr. Webster, 41, was attacked two years ago in an area of Stanley Park frequented by gay men looking for anonymous sex.

Crown lawyer Sandra Dworkin had recommended a sentence of 20 to 32 months in custody for the youth, now 19.

But Judge Romilly said that was not enough.

"He was part of a thug brigade stalking innocent victims for their own entertainment," he told the court as members of the young man's family looked on.

"This was an egregious and extremely violent act. It warrants a sentence that must reflect the abhorrence of civilized society at such a heinous crime."

Three years—two in custody and one under outside supervision—is the maximum punishment for manslaughter provided by the Youth Criminal Justice Act. After the sentence was imposed, the youth, who cannot be identified, was led away in handcuffs by court sheriffs. He showed no emotion.

Judge Romilly rejected Crown submissions that the beating of Mr. Webster was not a hate crime, based on the youth's claim that he and his friends were not looking for gays. Rather, the teenager told police, they were out to get "peeping toms" who spied on couples in cars parked at Stanley Park.

The judge noted that Mr. Webster was naked, except for socks and shoes, when he was savagely attacked and wondered how the attackers could be so naïve as to fail to notice they were in an area of Stanley Park "frequented" by gays.

And even if the youth were believed, an act demonstrating hatred toward peeping toms was also a hate crime, Judge Romilly said.

According to the youth's confession to police, the group of Burnaby teenagers went to Stanley Park after having a lot to drink "looking for those peeping-tom guys." As they had on three previous visits, they hid in the bushes, armed with bats and golf clubs.

"We saw him [Mr. Webster] there naked. I ran after him and I hit him," he recounted. Others in the group then killed the victim as he lay unconscious on the ground.[7]

Chapter Eight
COMMON DRIVING VIOLATIONS AND CAR ACCIDENTS

● ● ● ● ● ● ● ●

61

Common Driving Violations and Car Accidents

In every state in the United States it is easy to obtain a driver's license. Just about anyone, regardless of their judgment, maturity, level of responsibility, intelligence, or attention span, can find themselves lawfully behind the wheel of a vehicle. It is a very scary thought as inattentive, distracted, or uncaring individuals can operate a powerful mass of metal under high speeds in crowded and unsafe conditions. Getting into a car is probably the most dangerous thing you do day in and day out. If you are the driver, you have to be aware of the tragic affects your poor decisions or lack of attention could have upon you and others.

Busted

Speeding to be in time to catch the bus to school is not a wise decision.

Energized to get to school, a teenager clocked driving at 93 mph told a deputy he had to get home in time to catch the school bus, police said. Porter Superior Court Judge Julia Jent sentenced the teen to ride the bus to school after an earlier speeding conviction, Porter County Sheriff's deputies said.

Ryan M. Henry, 18, of Porter Township near Valparaiso in northwest Indiana, was caught speeding in a 45 mph zone Tuesday morning, police said.

Henry appeared to accelerate after passing a marked squad car, then turned into a driveway and shut off the lights to his 2001 Mustang, said Porter County Sheriff's Deputy Roger Bowles, who ticketed Henry.

Henry told Bowles that he had gone to a gas station to buy an energy drink and didn't want to miss the school bus. [1]

Why is it that many of us stop thinking when we get behind the wheel of a car? That is the time to be more cautious and thoughtful, not less.

Busted

You would think it was sound common sense not to drive illegally to your driving test.

A teenager is being charged with violating the Road Traffic Law in Nagoya, Japan, after riding his mother's motorbike to get his own motorcycle license.

Police said the 16-year old boy rode his mother's small motorbike to a driving school in Nagoya to try and get his license.

An investigative report on the incident was sent to prosecutors. [2]

Common Driving Violations

- Driving without a license
- Driving without a registration
- Driving without insurance
- Driving under the influence (DUI)
- Illegal U-turn
- Leaving the scene of an accident
- Hit and run
- Running a red light
- Running a stop sign
- Speeding
- Unlawful vehicle modification

62

Teenage Driving Risks Stats

Automobile accidents are the leading cause of death of teen-agers, accounting for one-third of all deaths in teens 16-18 years of age.

- Teens are 4 times more likely to be involved in an auto-mobile accident than older drivers, based on the number of miles driven.
- The death rate for male drivers involved in automobile accidents, ages 16-19, is twice that of female drivers.
- The presence of passengers increases the risk: of teens killed in automobile accidents, 45% had a youth passenger. The number of passengers in the vehicle increases the risk.
- Of teen deaths, 39% involve speeding.
- Teens have the lowest rate of seat belt use of any age group.
- Most teen deaths occur on weekends: 54% occurred on Friday, Saturday, and Sunday.
- 42% occurred between the hours of 9 P.M. and 6 A.M.
- Teen life style promotes drowsiness, a high risk factor in driving.[3]

Other Driving Violations

Most states have laws that prohibit the following conduct while driving:

Cell Phones: Some cities and states now prohibit the use of handheld phones while driving on certain roads or all roads. Do not use a cell phone while driving unless you can do so hands free. (Please see page 66).

Reckless Driving: You cannot operate your motor vehicle anywhere—on a street, parking lot, or parking structure—in a reckless disregard for the safety or property of others.

Road Rage: Do not try to retaliate if you are cut off by another car or another driver does something else to upset you. If you engage in road rage by trying to take matters into your own hands, you can have your license suspended or even end up in jail.

Littering and Throwing Objects from a Vehicle: It is usually a misde-meanor to throw anything from your car or at something from your car.

Lighted Cigarettes: In many areas it is illegal and subjects you to a fine if you throw a lighted ciga-rette from a motor vehicle. It is also an incredibly unwise thing to do in very arid regions of the country where blazing wild fires can result.

Drag Races. If you conduct drag or speed races, your driver's license can be suspended.

Do not do things while driving that will endanger others.

Unattended Child in a Vehicle: It is usually unlawful to leave a child under the age of 6 in a motor vehicle unattended by a person at least 12 years of age.

Laser Pointers: In many states it is now illegal to point a laser at an-other vehicle to harass or annoy anyone in another vehicle.

Seat Belts/Child Restraints: All persons must be in proper seat belt restraints before the vehicle can be lawfully oper-ated. New Hampshire is the only state that does not have a law requiring people over 18 to wear a seat belt.

Children 6 years or under, or under sixty (60) pounds, must be secured in federally approved safety seats. They must be placed in the back seat unless there is no back seat or the back seat is occupied by others less than 12 years of age.

Usually babies under one year old or weighing less than twenty (20) pounds are not allowed to be in a front seat that has an active air bag.

Joy Riding

Joy-riding: is generally defined as the taking of a car, boat, or other vehicle without the owner's permission, with no particular goal—a ride taken solely for pleasure or excitement.

In most states this violation is subject to a $1,000 fine and up to two (2) years in jail.

Speeding

Speed limits are posted on traffic signs on the sides of roads and highways. If you do not see a posted limit, as a general rule you should not exceed:

- 15 miles per hour in school zones
- 25 miles per hour in cities and towns
- 45 miles per hour on county and state roads
- 55-65 miles per hour on interstates, turnpikes, and freeways

As Fast as is Safe

Even if there is a posted speed limit you should always drive as fast as is safe under the prevailing conditions.

Be especially careful driving in snow, fog, heavy rain, and heavy traffic as you can be cited for improper driving even if you are not exceeding the posted speed limit under those conditions.

TWOC
Twolling
Twoccers

In England, joy rides are called TWOC (Taken Without Owner's Consent) and joy riders and borrowers are called Twoccers.[4]

Busted

Admitting to taking snowmobiles from private property for joy riding, two teens were arrested and charged with unauthorized use of a vehicle.[5]

Alaska Teen Charged as Adult in East Side Road Rage Stabbing.

The fact that you are under 18 years old may not protect you from being punished as an adult.

A 17-year-old accused of stabbing a man in a road rage incident Friday has been charged as an adult with first-degree assault, the Alaska district attorney's office said.

David Christopher Kellum is also charged with four counts of reckless endangerment, all misdemeanors, according to documents filed in court Saturday.

Kellum is accused of stabbing 52-year-old Johnnie F. Bowen with a folding knife Friday evening around rush hour, within sight of Anchorage, Alaska, Police Department headquarters. Bowen suffered lacerations to his spleen and diaphragm, and required surgery. He was recovering in the hospital Monday.

According to Alaska police and charging documents, Kellum was driving recklessly in his mother's 2003 silver Dodge Durango before the stabbing. Three passengers in the Durango told police that Kellum was speeding, tailgating, swerving in and out of traffic, honking his horn, flipping off drivers, and flashing his high beams, charges say.

Bowen, who was driving his 13-year-old son to hockey practice at the Tesoro Sports Centre, said he noticed the Durango as he drove down Tudor Road in his pickup. He told his son, "Don't ever drive like that."

Before long, the Durango started riding Bowen's bumper.

"Each time Mr. Bowen attempted to change lanes the defendant would also change lanes," charges say.

Bowen stopped at a red light…in front of the Alaska Police Department. The Durango pulled up behind him and the driver blew the horn and started flashing the high beams, charges say.

Bowen said in a telephone interview from his hospital room Monday that he was not sure what was going on in the Durango at that point. He thought there might have been a medical emergency. He got out of his pickup, walked over to the driver's side window and tapped on the glass.

"Is there something I can help you with?" he asked the man. "What's the problem?"

"I'll show you what my problem is," Bowen recalled the driver saying back.

Kellum attacked Bowen as Bowen started walking back to his pickup…Bowen was stabbed once in the side and then got control of the knife.

The three passengers inside the Durango—a mother and her daughter and another male—saw the two men struggle, charges say. The daughter tried to get into the driver's seat of the Durango, but Kellum returned and pushed her away…

Kellum drove off. The passengers told Alaska police that they pleaded with him to let them out of the truck but that he refused to stop and locked all the doors, charges say. Kellum threatened to "take them all out" if they went to the authorities, the mother told police.[6]

Maximum Prison Sentence for Teen in South Philadelphia Road Rage Murder.

A Philadelphia judge has imposed the maximum sentence on a 19-year-old man for shooting a 14-year-old boy to death during a road rage incident last summer in South Philadelphia.

Defendant Charles Meyers…has been sentenced to 26-52 years in prison for the third-degree murder verdict…

Tykeem Law was riding a bicycle with some friends when along came Meyers in a car. According to the prosecutor, Meyers shot Law because the boy did not get his bike out of the way fast enough.

And it cost him his life. Now, it will cost Meyers a good part of his life.

In court on Friday, Meyers said he was sorry and would even trade places with the victim if he could.

During the trial the defense had contended that Meyers had acted in self-defense after Law reached under his tee-shirt. Meyers' attorney said his client thought Law was reaching for a gun and reacted.

But no gun was found—Law had been unarmed.[7]

Cell Phone Driving Laws as of 2010

Current state cell phone driving law highlights include the following:

- **Handheld Cell Phone Bans:** Six states (California, Connecticut, New Jersey, New York, Oregon, and Washington), the District of Columbia, and the Virgin Islands have laws prohibiting driving while talking on handheld cell phones. The list is growing rapidly, so you should check your local and state law.
- **All Cell Phone Bans:** No state completely bans all types of cell phone use (handheld and hands-free) for all drivers, but many prohibit cell phone use by certain segments of the population.
- **Novice Drivers:** Twenty-four states and the District of Columbia ban all cell use by novice drivers.
- **Text Messaging:** Twenty-three states and the District of Columbia have a text messaging ban for all drivers.
- **Novice Drivers:** An additional eight states prohibit text messaging by novice drivers.[8]

Teen Driving Stats

The most common distraction for drivers is the use of cell phones. Talking or listening on a handheld device increased the risk of a crash or near crash 1.3 times. Dialing a hand-held device increased the risk of a crash or near crash by almost three times.

Nearly 80% of crashes and 65% of near crashes involved some form of driver inattention within three seconds before the event.[9]

Teen Driver Stats

Deaths
Each year more than 5,000 teens ages 16 to 20 die from fatal injuries caused by car accidents. About 400,000 drivers aged 16 to 20 will be seriously injured.

Risks
The risk of being involved in a car accident is the highest for drivers aged 16 to 19 years. Higher than any other age group. For each mile driven, teen drivers aged 16 to 19 years old are about four times more likely than other drivers to crash.

Stats
Teenagers are about 10 percent of the U.S. population but account for 12 percent of all fatal car crashes.

Costs
Drivers (both male and female) under age 24 account for 30%—$26 billion dollars—of the total costs of car accidents in the U.S.

Male vs. Female

The car accident death rate for male teen drivers and passengers is more than one and a half times that of female teen drivers (19.4 killed per 100,000 male drivers compared with 11.1 killed per 100,000 female drivers).

New Drivers

The risk of a car crash is much higher during the first year teenagers are able to drive.

Alcohol

About 23% of drivers aged 15 to 20 who died in car crashes had a blood alcohol count of 0.08 or higher.

About 30% of teens reported that within the previous 30 days, they had been a passenger in a car with a driver who had been drinking alcohol. One in 10 teens said that they personally had driven after drinking alcohol.

Of teen drivers killed in auto crashes after drinking and driving, 74% did not wear a seat belt. [10]

Driving Tips

Teens are generally inexperienced and tend to make more driving mistakes. Although you may feel comfortable behind the wheel, driving experience takes time and practice. You should follow these tips while driving:

- Always be alert when driving—keep you eyes and ears open.
- Stay focused on your driving. Don't be distracted by passengers, the radio, or a cell phone.
- Always wear your seatbelt. Seatbelts can reduce the risk of fatal accidents.
- Do not drink and drive—statistics show that 60% of teenagers involved in auto accidents have been drinking. [11]

Registration and Car Insurance

In most states, vehicles using public roads must be registered each year with your state Department of Motor Vehicles (DMV). Check the vehicle regulations in your state.

In some states, vehicles must be inspected each year. In others, they must be smog certified every few years.

In some states, if your car insurance is cancelled or lapses for non-payment, your car registration and plates will be suspended and you can no longer drive your car. [12]

Busted

Do not compound your legal problems by further reckless disregard of the law.

Paris Hilton was sentenced to 45 days in jail last week for violating her probation on a previous DUI-related conviction. In February, police pulled over Hilton on Sunset Boulevard, driving at a "high rate of speed" with a suspended license. In court, Hilton said she didn't know her license was suspended. "I'm sorry, and I did not do it on purpose at all," she told the judge. But, according to the Los Angeles city attorney's office, Hilton had been notified twice of the suspension by police and sent a notice by the DMV. "We had a very strong case," says spokesman Frank Mateljan. [13]

67

Car Accidents: Hit And Run

If you are in a car accident:
- You must stop as soon as possible without endangering traffic.
- If you hit an unoccupied car you must leave your name and address on a note on the car you hit.
- If you hit someone's property on or off the road, you must search for the owner to provide your name and address
- If someone is hurt in a car accident, you must offer assistance and call the police and/or ambulance
- Exchange with the other driver:
  - Your names and addresses
  - Driver's license numbers
  - Car registration numbers
  - Car insurance company names, phone numbers, and policy numbers.

Leaving the Scene of an Accident

If you leave the scene of an accident where someone was injured, killed, or there was property damage without exchanging the above information, you can be subject to criminal prosecution. This is a very serious offense—do not leave the scene of an accident.

Notifying the Police

In most states, any accident resulting in injury, death, or over $1,000 of property damage must be immediately reported to the police.

You must fill out an official accident report with the police within forty-eight (48) hours of the accident.

Teens Need Driving Restrictions

There is sound reason insurance companies charge much more to insure teen drivers.

A study from the University of Michigan Transportation Research Institute found little improvement in the rate of teen car crashes over the past 15 years. It calls for more restrictive licensing for teen drivers in Michigan and other states, the *Detroit Free Press* (freep. com) reported.

The study found teens were 2-1/2 times as likely as adults to be in a car crash and that the likelihood of a crash increased when teens had passengers, specifically teen passengers, and when they drove at night or weekends. The risk increases when factors are combined.

"Inexperience, underdeveloped driving skills, and immaturity together contribute to poor performance of driving tasks, UM-TRI researcher C. Raymond Bingham said.[14]

What To Do if You Have a Car Accident

- Get medical help for anyone who may be injured.
- Call the police and follow their instruction. If you are in an unsafe area, you may relocate to the nearest police station or public place and then call the police.
- Get names, addresses, driver's license numbers, telephone numbers, and insurance information of anyone involved in or witnessing the accident.
- Call your parents or guardian and tell them what has happened and where you are located.
- Notify your insurance agent or insurance company.[15]

Emergency Car Information

Keep the following information in a safe place in your vehicle for ready reference in the event of an emergency:
- Insurance Company
- Policy Number
- Agent's Name
- Agent's Phone Number
- Police Department Phone Number
- Towing Company
- Towing Company Phone Number

Busted

Another senseless act of road rage.

Richardson police have charged a teenager in connection with a fatal Christmas Eve crash they say resulted because of road rage.

According to investigators, Gabriel Gaona was racing his black Jaguar against another vehicle at about 4 P.M., when a crash occurred that killed an innocent man.

The alleged incident began at Arapaho and Plano roads where witnesses said a white Pontiac G6 refused to allow the Jaguar to pass.

Police said the two cars sped eastbound on Arapaho Road at speeds up to 80 mph when the Pontiac, driven by 40-year-old Philip Cullens, struck a blue Ford Escape as it exited the Block Apartments.

The sport utility driver, 31-year-old Christopher Cain Soliz, was taken by CareFlite helicopter to Baylor Dallas where he later died. His 34-year-old passenger, Amy Burns, was treated and released at Parkland Hospital.

Gaona's Jaguar avoided the collision but left the road, and damaged surrounding landscaping and property.

Gaona is charged with criminally negligent manslaughter. Cullens, who was hospitalized at Parkland with non-life threatening injuries, will face the same charge, police said.[16]

Teen Driving Stats

According to the Youth Driver Research Initiative in Texas:

The vast majority of crashes involving young drivers are caused by just five factors, and drinking is at the bottom of the list. They are:
- Driving at night
- Distractions (other teen passengers, loud music, text messages)
- Speeding
- Not wearing safety belts
- Alcohol[17]

Chapter Nine
PARTIES AND PARTYING

Parties and Partying

Throwing a party or attending a party can subject you to legal and personal safety issues if you are not vigilant as to the guests (both invited and uninvited ones), the activities (use of drugs and alcohol), ages of sex partners, consumption of alcohol by underage drinkers, and damage to property.

Any party can be dispersed by the police and can be a violation of your local or state partying codes if there is:
- Fighting
- Rowdiness
- Alcohol and drug use
- Loud noise such as music at a loud level or inappropriate shouting in public at any time
- Anything that generally disturbs the peace.
- A nuisance to your neighbors caused by:
  - Trash and litter
  - Public urination
  - Vandalism
- Underage drinking
- Selling of alcohol or drugs
- Loitering
- Obstruction of a highway
- An offensive utterance, gesture, or display in a public place
- A display of a deadly weapon in a public place in a manner calculated to alarm
- Or, if the hour is late.[1]

Interference with Police Officers

No person can use or threaten to use physical interference or to knowingly obstruct, impair, or hinder any police officer, fire fighter, city employee, or other public official.

If you have been ordered to move by a police officer, you must not remain in the officer's presence, disrupt, obstruct, hinder, or impair the officer.

Carrying or Drinking Alcohol in Public

You cannot have open containers or consume any alcohol in any vehicle, public place, school, or university.

New Orleans is one of the few cities in the United States where you can drink alcohol on the street.

Trespass

It is unlawful for you to enter a vehicle or property of another without a legal privilege, or to enter a place restricted by gender (e.g. restrooms, locker rooms, etc.)

Party Crashers

Party crashers are technically trespassers if they are uninvited, so the police may be requested to throw them out.

Busted

Even if you are old enough to purchase alcohol, do not provide it to minors or you will face serious legal exposure.

Grapevine police have arrested two teens for furnishing alcohol to minors during beer parties this past weekend. Police say more than 50 teens attended the bashes and officers issued 14 citations to juveniles for drinking alcohol. Lt. Todd Dearing says parents were out of town during both parties and officers happened upon the homes. Lt. Todd Dearing says police arrested the 17-year-old daughter of one of the homeowners for supplying the booze for a Friday night party. Lt. Dearing says it was easy to spot with all the plastic cups and beer cans in the yard.

The same thing happened Saturday night, when police arrested another teen at his home. The teens face a $4,000 fine and a year in jail.[2]

Party Ground Rules

If you have a party, you should keep the following guidelines in mind:

- Limit the number of people you invite.
- Only invite people you know.
- Always serve food if you plan to serve alcohol.
- Make non-alcoholic beverages available and visible.
- Serve drinks in plastic/paper cups to avoid glass breakage.
- Keep the noise level down as much as possible.
- Limit the number of drinks served per person.
- Never serve alcohol to an already intoxicated person.
- Help people find rides home from a sober driver who has not consumed any alcohol.
- Do not drink too much yourself so you can stay in control of your own party or designate/be a sober host.
- Do not sell alcohol.
- Know the signs of alcohol poisoning and what to do to keep friends safe.
- Be prepared to have overly intoxicated guests stay all night if no safe transportation is available.
- Do not allow drinking contests or drinking games that encourage the over-consumption of alcohol.
- Abide by all local state and federal laws so that you and your guests will not get into trouble.
- Check with your landlord about their policies regarding parties or gatherings—read your lease.
- Do not provide alcohol to underage people.
- Get to know your (adult) neighbors and let them know when you are planning a party.
- Have guests park legally (not on lawns) or risk getting towed.
- Stop serving alcohol an hour before the end of a party; make sure there is still food and non-alcoholic drinks available. When alcohol is gone it is easier to break up a party.
- Keep your neighbors happy: Clean up after the party and pick up trash outside of your apartment/house.[3]

Call 911 for emergencies. If you need help breaking up a party that has become out of control, it is wise to call the police and ask for assistance—before they come on their own or before a neighbor has complained.

Ground Rules for a Party Guest

When you attend a party:

- You do not have to drink alcohol.
- Have a plan for transportation ready before you go out. If you plan to drink, do not take your car to the party or bar.
- If you are over 21 and choose to drink alcoholic beverages, keep your consumption moderate (0 drinks if you are driving, 1 per

Busted

Do not compound your poor choices by blatantly violating the law.

A group of teenagers face criminal charges after they illegally used a rental property to throw a party Saturday night, according to the Walton County Sheriff's Office. The Sheriff's Office arrested fourteen juveniles and three adult teens after a deputy found them partying at a rental property on County Road 30A, according to a news release. Their names were not released. The suspects took the rental property's front door off its hinges to enter the unit, the release stated. The door was found later that night on a boardwalk near the beach. All the suspects have been charged with felony counts of burglary and fraud (defrauding an innkeeper), and a misdemeanor count each of criminal mischief, the release said.[4]

hour is a safe pace, and no more than 3 per night is best).

- If you are drinking, also eat food. Eat before you go out.
- Attend with a friend and look out for each other.
- Leave your valuables at home. Carry only the ID and the money you will need that night.
- If you choose to be sexually active, bring and use condoms.
- Stay off all roofs and any balcony that is crowded.
- Do not play with fire.
- Do not argue with cops.
- Remember drugs and alcohol do not mix—even over-the-counter and prescription drugs can be very dangerous when combined with alcohol.
- Avoid behavior that might get your hosts in trouble—such as sneaking a drink to someone underage, carrying alcoholic drinks onto public property, throwing bottles, etc.
- Treat your hosts, their home, and their other guests with respect.
- Obey requests from hosts to quiet down, leave, or stop drinking.[5]

Social Host Liability

You and your parents should be warned that social host liability laws are being passed throughout the country. These laws hold parents—and sometimes, older siblings or other legally aged adults—accountable for hosting underage drinking events.

Underage Drinking

Social host liability laws hold adults who serve or provide alcohol to underage people criminally liable if that minor is killed or injured, or if that minor kills or injures someone else. The laws can also extend to parents who do not take sufficient measures to prevent underage drinking in their homes, even if they are not home when the drinking occurs. Parents can be charged for medical bills and property damage or sued for emotional pain and suffering, depending on how the specific laws are interpreted in your state.

73

Teen Drinking Stats

Two thirds of teens who drink get their alcohol from parents or other adults, according to the 2003 National Academy of Sciences Report. "Some parents believe that it's safer for their teens to drink at home than to drink anywhere else," according to the U.S. Department of Health and Human Services Substance Abuse and mental Health Services Administration. Yet the responsibility can rest squarely on parents' shoulders if something goes wrong, as it too often does. For instance, a Pennsylvania parent was sentenced to a 1 to 4-1/2 year prison term for involuntary manslaughter after allowing underage students to drink at a party the parent hosted. Three students died in a drunk-driving accident after the party.[7]

Connecticut has a law that allows misdemeanor charges to be filed against adults who knowingly allow anyone under 21 to possess alcohol on their property. You should review the details of your state laws to see how social host liability is interpreted.[8]

Busted

Many adults are going to prison for supplying alcohol to underage drinkers even within their own homes. If your parents are not willing to act intelligently and responsibly, you should.

Two American parents have started a two-year prison sentence for serving $350 worth of beer and other alcohol at their son's 16th birthday party.

The drinking age in the United States is 21, but Elisa Kelly, 42, and George Robinson, 52, decided to buy alcohol for their son Ryan's party, which was attended by about 30 people—between 12 and 18 years old—on August 16, 2002.

Concerned that the teenagers would drink without supervision, the parents said they had bought alcohol with the understanding that the teens would spend the night at their place and collected half a dozen car keys to prevent drunk driving.[9]

Busted

Tragic events can result from a parent trying to be a "good guy" or "with-it" parent, but no apparent good deed goes unpunished.

A woman who authorities say provided alcohol to juveniles at a party last November has been arrested and charged with manslaughter in the death of a 16-year-old boy who succumbed to acute alcohol intoxication sometime during the night of the party.

Thirty-nine-year old Bridget Carolyn Parmer has already posted a $10,000 bond after her arrest Monday.

Parmer told authorities that she went to bed around 2 or 3 A.M. and was not aware that teens were drinking vodka at the party in her home.[10]

Riots and Rioting

A riot is a public disturbance involving three or more people whose conduct creates a danger of damage or injury to people or property or substantially obstructs the performance of any government function.

You can be fined and/or jailed for:
- Inciting a riot: urging a group of five or more people to engage in a riot
- Arming a riot: providing a deadly or destructive weapon (Please see Chapter Four) to someone to use in a riot
- Engaging in a riot

College Ban

In some states if you are convicted of engaging in a riot you will not be allowed to attend any state colleges or universities for at least one year.

Chapter Nine
GRAFFITI

● ● ● ● ● ● ● ●

Graffiti

Unfortunately, almost anywhere you travel today in the world you can observe graffiti on any immoveable object, even marring local and historical landmarks. One wonders what compels a person to desecrate a building that has stood for centuries, survived wars, storms, and floods only to be savaged by an uncaring person that wants to leave his or her mark in a public place for personal ego, gang-related behavior, or no reason.

Crime

You should be aware that graffiti is vandalism and a crime. It is destruction of property. This crime can be either a misdemeanor or felony, depending on the value of the property destroyed.

Restitution

A judge may and should order you to pay the cost of the damage you caused.

Types Of Graffiti

Some jurisdictions go so far as to break down graffiti into different categories, such as:
1. Hip-Hop
2. Gang
3. Hate Crime
4. Folk Epigraphy (the writings of a common man, i.e. "Freud was here")
5. Political Activism (such as "End the War")
6. Stencil
7. Latrinalia – bathroom graffiti
8. Satanic[1]

Malicious Destruction Of Property

It is a crime to damage someone's property intentionally. If you intentionally break the windshield of your friend's car or commit graffiti, this crime is called malicious destruction of property.

Punishment can be up to two (2) years in jail.

Busted

Do not let peer pressure or just poor judgment place you in a position to violate the law.

Police have busted a teen graffiti gang that has been posting internet challenges encouraging other kids to do battle with paint and become "King of the Mountain."

Barrett Township Police filed criminal charges this week against Amy Young, 18, of Pocono Pines, PA, and three juveniles. The arrests came after a five-month investigation.[2]

Graffiti Stats

According to the city of San Antonio, Texas:
- It costs America more than $8 billion per year just to clean up graffiti.
- It is a common misperception that most graffiti is done by gangs when in fact gangs are responsible for less than 10% of graffiti.
- Graffiti vandals represent every social, ethnic, and economic background. Suburban males commit approximately 50% of graffiti vandalism from pre-teen to early 20s.
- The average age of the arrested graffiti vandal is 17-18.
- There are four primary motivating factors for graffiti vandalism: fame, rebellion, self-expression, and power
- Getting the media to publish photos and air videotape of graffiti is often the ultimate fame for graffiti vandals.[2]

Busted

You might call it a self-fulfilling prophecy.

It is six months in jail for a Mariners Harbor teen who ranged across Staten Island plastering his graffiti tag, "Jerky," on just about anything stationary—storefronts, concrete barriers, train trestles, utility poles, bus shelters, and FDNY call boxes.

The sentence that Stapleton Criminal County Judge Matthew A. Sciarrino, Jr. slapped on Corey Rosalli, 18, is among the toughest imposed in recent memory for a graffiti conviction, court observers said.

Last year, Sciarrino sentenced graffiti scourge Russell Farriola of West Brighton, whom cops labeled "public enemy No. 1," to six months behind bars.

Bagged after a yearlong probe, Farriola allegedly defaced dumpsters, cemetery fences, cars, street signs, a political campaign headquarters, and private property with his tag, "Aloe."

On Tuesday, Rosalli pleaded guilty to a misdemeanor count of making graffiti.

He had been arrested October 15 and charged with 57 graffiti incidents dating to December 2006.

Officers from the Citywide Vandals Task Force collared Rosalli as he left Stapleton Criminal Court after a proceeding in another graffiti case.

Sciarrino also sentenced Rosalli to six months behind bars in connection with a May 21 graffiti arrest. He previously had pleaded guilty in that matter and was awaiting sentencing. His arrest last week violated the terms of that plea deal.[5]

Busted

Virtually everyone is tired of seeing graffiti plastered everywhere.

A judge on Wednesday sentenced a 17-year-old man to jail time, probation, a fine, and community service, saying she was fed up with seeing graffiti in the city.

Gabriel Martinez pleaded guilty to a graffiti charge in connection with damaging Moody High School property. Police also suspect him of damaging city signs, several residential fences, and a fire hydrant, although he has not been charged in those cases.

"I was being a bonehead," Martinez said when asked by his attorney, Randy Pretzer, why he did it.

Prosecutor Doug Mann said Martinez was part of a local graffiti tagging crew that is in constant competition with another crew.

The fences that were damaged have been tagged several times with the street names of members from both crews, Mann added.

Watts sentenced Martinez to six months in the Nueces County Jail, three years probation, a $1,500 fine, and 150 hours of community service, which he must serve by cleaning up graffiti.

"I find this to be a plague on our community," Watts said before imposing the sentence.

After his release from jail, Martinez also must follow a 8 P.M. curfew for another six months.[4]

Chapter Eleven
ALCOHOL, DRUG, AND TOBACCO-RELATED ISSUES

● ● ● ● ● ● ● ●

Alcohol, Drug, and Tobacco-Related Legal Issues

All states have a minimum purchase age of 21 for alcoholic beverages. It is 18 years of age in Puerto Rico, the U.S. Virgin Islands, and Guam.

Unlawful

It is unlawful for anyone to sell alcohol to, to make alcohol available, or to purchase alcohol for anyone under 21 years of age. So, do not buy alcohol and then provide it to underage people, the consequences can be severe.

Drinking Alcohol

You must be at least 21 years old to consume, possess, or purchase beer, wine, liquor, or any other alcoholic drink.

Penalties

Penalties for underage use of alcohol varies by state, but it is common for underage possession of alcohol to be classified as a misdemeanor with fines up to $2,500 and jail time up to one year.

In some states, if you are convicted of alcohol possession under the age of 21, you can:
- Be fined
- Be required to perform community service
- Have your driver's license suspended

Underage Presence Where Alcohol is Served

If you are underage, in most states you can be in a place where alcohol is served if:
- You lawfully work at that establishment
- You are with a parent
- You are with a guardian
- You are with a spouse who is of lawful drinking age
- There are no alcoholic items being served, consumed or given away during the designated time you are there
- You are there to buy food or non-alcoholic beverages and leave the establishment immediately after you purchased these items
- You attend public facilities, sporting events, restaurants, and similar locations where alcohol is served[1]

Busted

Avoid the immature and irresponsible temptation to throw a party when your parents are out of town.

A booze-filled party at a Chappaqua, NY, home has led to the arrest of the teen who hosted the bash while her parents were out of town.

Police, responding to a noise complaint at the home on Devoe Road Saturday night, found more than 50 teens at the residence. They also found beer and vodka bottles scattered everywhere, as well as one unconscious 16-year-old-girl.

She had to be taken to a local hospital.

The owner of the home is defending his daughter. He told the *Journal News* that it appears she invited only a few friends over, but members of the football team showed up uninvited, and forced their way in.[2]

Underage Drinking and Drunk Driving Stats

Alcohol-related consequences for college students between the ages of 18-24:
- Death: 1,700 die each year from alcohol-related unintentional injuries, including motor vehicle crashes.
- Injury: 599,000 are unintentionally injured under the influence of alcohol.
- Assault: More than 606,000 are assaulted by another student who has been drinking.
- Sexual Abuse: More than 97,000 are victims of alcohol-related sexual assault or date rape.
- Unsafe Sex: 400,000 have unprotected sex and more than 100,000 report having been too intoxicated to know if they consented to having sex.
- Academic Problems: About 25 percent of students report academic consequences of their drinking including missing class, falling behind, doing poorly on exams or papers, and receiving lower grades overall.
- Health Problems/Suicide Attempts: More than 150,000 develop an alcohol-related health problem.
- Drunk Driving: 1.2 million drive under the influence of alcohol each year.
- Nearly half (48%) of all of the alcohol consumed by students attending 4-year colleges is consumed by underage students.
- Approximately 6% of college students have been diagnosed as alcohol dependent and nearly one-third of students would be given an alcohol abuse diagnosis under psychiatric criteria. Approximately 44% of students reported at least one symptom of either abuse or dependence.[3]

Drugs and Alcohol Stats

- Nearly half of America's full-time college students abuse drugs or binge drink at least once a month. For college gun owners, the rate of binge drinking is even higher—two-thirds.
- Plus, college gun owners are more likely than the average student to:
- Engage in binge drinking
- Need an alcoholic drink first thing in the morning
- Use cocaine or crack
- Be arrested for a DUI
- Vandalize property
- Get in trouble with police.[4]

Teen Alcohol Stats

- More than 40% of teens who admitted drinking said they drink when they are upset
- 31% said they drink alone
- 25% said they drink when they are bored
- 25% said they drink to "get high"

Each year, students spend $5.5 billion on alcohol, more than they spend on soft drinks, tea, milk, juice, coffee, or books combined. On a typical campus, per capita student spending for alcohol—$446 per student—far exceeds the per capita budget of the college library.

Approximately 240,000 to 360,000 of the nation's 12 million current undergraduates will ultimately die from alcohol-related causes—more than the number that will be MAs and PhDs combined.

Sixty percent (60%) of college women diagnosed with a sexually transmitted disease were drunk at the time of infection.

Eight (8) young people a day die in alcohol-related crashes.[5]

Teen Stats

In 2005, about 10.8 million people from 12-20 years old (28.2% of this age group) reported drinking alcohol in the past month. Nearly 7.2 million (18.8%) were binge drinkers, and 2.3 million (6.0%) were heavy drinkers.

3 Out of 4

Three out of every four students (75%) have consumed alcohol (more than just a few sips) by the end of high school.

College Bingers

Young adults between 18 and 22 years old and enrolled full-time in college were more likely than their peers not enrolled full time to use alcohol in the past month, to binge drink, and to drink heavily.

High School Seniors

More than half (58%) of 12th graders report having been drunk at least once in their life and one-fifth (20%) of 8th graders report having been drunk at least once in their life.

Teen Drinking and Driving Stats

Twenty-eight percent (28%) of 15-20-year-old drivers who were killed in motor vehicle crashes in 2005 had been drinking.

Driving Impaired: Unrestrained

Drivers are less likely to use seat belts when they have been drinking. In 2005, 64% of young passenger vehicle drivers who had been drinking and involved in fatal crashes were unrestrained. Of the young drivers who had been drinking and were killed in crashes, 74% were unrestrained.

28.5%

During the last 30 days, 28.5% of high school students nationwide had ridden one or more times in a car or other vehicle driven by someone who had been drinking alcohol.

39%

In 2005, 39% of fatal crashes (all age groups) involved alcohol. The rate of alcohol involvement in fatal crashes is more than three times higher at night than during the day (59% vs. 18%).[6]

Tobacco

In most states, if you are under 18 years of age, you cannot purchase any tobacco products.[7] Common tobacco products are:

- Cigarettes
- Cigarette tobacco
- Smokeless tobacco
- Loose-leaf chewing tobacco
- Plug chewing tobacco
- Twist chewing tobacco
- Moist snuff
- Dry snuff

Criminal Penalties

Do not buy or provide tobacco products for anyone under 18. A minor that uses or buys tobacco can be subject to criminal penalties, as could the person that provides tobacco to a person less than 18 years of age.

Teen Smoking Stats

Teen smoking had been on a sharp decline since the mid- to late 1990s, but subsequent data shows that the adolescent smoking rates are rising slightly.

According to a 2005 study done by the Center for Disease Control (CDC), 23% of high school students reported smoking cigarettes in the last month. This is compared with a 2003 study of high school students that showed 21.9% of high school students reported smoking.

The CDC study showed that 80% of smokers begin before the age of 18. A similar study published by the American Lung Association website shows 90% of smokers begin before the age of 21.

A study that was done by the CDC also found some interesting facts and estimates:
1. About 3,900 teens younger than 18 start smoking each day.
2. Of the 3,900 teens that start smoking each day, 1,500 will become regular smokers.
3. Those who smoke often have secondary behavioral issues such as violence, drug/alcohol use, and high-risk sexual behavior. [8]

Half (50%) of American young people have tried cigarettes by 12th grade.

Young adults between 18 and 25 years old had the highest rate of current use of a tobacco product, 44.3%.[9]

Teen Tobacco Stats

- Nearly all first use of tobacco occurs before high school graduation.
- Most young people who smoke are addicted to nicotine and report that they want to quit but are unable to do so.
- Tobacco is often the first drug used by young people who use alcohol and illegal drugs.
- Among young people, those with poorer grades and lower self images are most likely to begin using tobacco.[10]

Cigarette Butt Litter: "A Plague on Our Planet"

Cigarettes are not only harmful to the smoker, but they are harmful to the environment.

According to Keep America Beautiful, Americans are smoking fewer cigarettes than ever before, yet cigarette butts continue to be the most commonly littered item in the United States and around the world today. They specify two reasons for this statistic—lack of awareness on the smoker's part and the lack of available waste receptacles at transition locations, such as outside stores and other buildings and public transportation pickup spots.

Cigarette Filters

The core of most cigarette filters—the part that looks like white cotton—is actually a form of plastic called cellulose acetate. By itself, cellulose acetate is very slow to degrade in our environment. Depending on the conditions of the area where the cigarette butt is discarded, it can take 18 months to 10 years for a cigarette filter to decompose. But that is not the worst of it. Used cigarette filters are full of toxins known as tar, and those chemicals leach into the ground and waterways, damaging living organisms that contact them. And, most filters are discarded with bits of tobacco still attached to them as well, further polluting our environment with nicotine.[11]

Teen Tobacco Stats

In the United States today, an average of 3,000 people quit smoking and another 1,200 die from smoking every single day of the year. With statistics like that, the tobacco industry must always be working to gain new recruits. That means finding ways to addict… teens, many of whom start smoking by 14, and more often than not become addicted by the time they are 19.[12]

Teen Smoking Stats

Approximately 80% of adult smokers started smoking before the age of 18. Every day, nearly 3,000 young people under the age of 18 become regular smokers.

More than 5 million children living today will die prematurely because of a decision they will make as adolescents—the decision to smoke cigarettes.[13]

Drug Paraphernalia

It is illegal to:
- Possess any equipment that can be used to make, use, or grow drugs (e.g., a roach clip).
- Be present where an illegal substance is being used.
- Help anyone use illegal substances. [14]

Busted

If you are foolish enough to violate the law, do not compound your foolishness by posting your illegal conduct for the world to see.

The *FdLReporter.com* (Fond du Lac, WI) reports that 18-year-old, Moua Yang, was arrested recently in Sheboygan, WI, for allegedly posting a picture of marijuana on his MySpace page with a caption that read "My Mary Jane thats growin in my closet right now."

Sheboygan police found his MySpace page while monitoring the web for gang activity. According to *FdLReporter.com*, police Lt. Dave Schafhauser was surprised at how brazen this young man and his cohorts were on the web. "They talked bout their growing of the marijuana and some of the gang activity they were involved in," said Schaufhauser.

Police arrested Yang earlier this week after they searched his house and found three potted marijuana plants in the basement closet. He is now facing felony charges for the manufacturing of marijuana and for maintaining a drug trafficking house. He also is charged with the misdemeanor offense of possession of marijuana and drug paraphernalia.[15]

Busted

Even an honors student has to be smart enough to evaluate the potential repercussions of his actions in advance.

An honors student has been charged with delivering marijuana-spiked muffins to a teachers' lounge in a senior prank that sent 18 people to the hospital and triggered an FBI and terrorism investigation.

"I had no idea of the scope of my actions," Ian Walker, 18, said Friday. He can receive 10 years in prison or more if convicted of felony charges.

Walker is accused of bringing adulterated bran muffins to Tellini's suburban school May 16 and claiming they were part of a Boy Scout project. When Lake Highlands High School employees ate the muffins, they began complaining of nausea, lightheadedness, and headaches.

Most of those sickened were quickly treated and released, but Rita Greenfield, an 86-year-old receptionist, spent two days in the hospital.

"They were just thinking it would be fun to get these teachers all silly and giggly," Greenfield said. "I do not think of this as a prank at all. It has caused heartaches and hard feelings."[16]

Growing Weed

Do not cultivate your own illegal drugs. And if you foolishly do so, do not post pictures of you with them on the Internet.

Why would anyone be clueless enough to advertise worldwide that they are breaking the law?

A California high school student thought it'd be cool. . .to post a picture of himself smoking pot out of a bong on MySpace. Unfortunately for Daniel Blanchard, a Placer County Deputy Sheriff came across the picture. This sheriff is also the School Resource Officer assigned to the teen's high school and called him into his office to talk about it. During questioning Blanchard's backpack was searched and found to contain marijuana, hashish, and a marijuana pipe. He was, of course, busted. It should be noted that the "it's not mine" defense is greatly weakened when the police are armed with a photo (that you supplied) hitting on a 20" bong. (Also, why Blanchard went to a meeting with a backpack full of pot is yet another unanswered question.)

In the old (pre-Internet) days, people didn't distribute pictures of themselves breaking the law. It was considered unwise. But in today's world anything online goes, people are posting pictures of themselves doing really stupid things.

By the way, Blanchard's bad day didn't stop with the backpack seizure. A subsequent search of Blanchard's car revealed more drugs, digital scales, packaging materials, bongs, four knives, more than a dozen hypodermic syringes, gun powder, and potassium nitrate. When deputies searched Blanchard's bedroom, they say they found more chemicals used in bomb making and several printed materials on making bombs, including the *Anarchist's Cookbook*.

I guess the good news is that Blanchard was smart enough not to post a picture of himself making a bomb—not that it mattered.[19]

Busted

Even what you may mistakenly believe is a minor or inconsequential action could result in more serious consequences, especially if a judge, prosecutor, or law enforcement official wants to make an example out of you.

In June 2004, 18-year-old Mitchell Lawrence was sentenced to two years in jail for selling a teaspoonful of marijuana to an undercover police officer for $20.00 in Massachusetts.[20]

Young Women Drink, Party, Post

Again, why would rational and intelligent people place items on the Internet that could damage their lives forever?

On a Facebook group that celebrates young women getting drunk, there's no such thing as going too far.

One young woman dances on top of a bar. Another sits on the toilet drinking a beer. Several vomit. One appears with a bruised and bandaged face ("I just got drunk and fell out of a car," she writes.) In another photo, two women urinate into a waterfall.

What you won't find on this page—called "Thirty Reasons Girls Should Call it a Night"—is humiliation and embarrassment. For the most part, the women post the photos themselves, seemingly with pride. This makes many adults—teachers, counselors, and parents—worry that students aren't thinking through the consequences of showing themselves drunk to the world.

Many photos on the site are accompanied by full names and the colleges the women attend, apparently without much concern that parents, or potential employers, will take a look.

"You can't overstate how unthinking these kids are at 18, 19, 20 years old," said Robert L. Carothers, president of the University of Rhode Island, and a former member of the National Institute on Alcohol Abuse and Alcoholism's Committee on Campus Drinking. "They're not a thoughtful bunch, by and large."…

Forty percent of college students binge drink, according to a report this year by the Center on Alcohol and Substance Abuse. The report lists many ramifications of college binge drinking, including injuries, sexual violence, and vandalism. In addition, college students who reported having considered suicide were more likely to be active binge drinkers.[21]

●　●　●　●　●　●　●　●

Teen Drug Stats

Marijuana is the most commonly used illicit drug in the nation (14.6 million past month users).

Half of teens (50%) have tried an illicit drug by the time they finish high school.

Nationwide, 25.4% of students had been offered, sold, or given an illegal drug by someone on school property during the 12 months preceding the survey.

Twenty-three percent (23%) of teens report that marijuana is easier to buy than cigarettes or beer.

The increase in the use of marijuana has been especially pronounced. Between 1992 and 2006, past-month use of marijuana increased from:
- 8% to 12% among high school seniors
- 8% to 14% among 10th graders
- 4% to 7% among 8th graders

Teen Ecstasy Stats

Twenty-three percent (23%) of teens know a friend or classmate who has used ecstasy.

Teen Prescription Stats

Twenty-six percent (26%) of teens know a friend or classmate who has abused prescription drugs. [17]

Teen Drug Stats: High School Seniors

Of high school seniors in 2006:
- 42.3% reported having ever used marijuana/hashish
- 8.5% reported having ever used cocaine
- 1.4% reported having ever used heroin[18]

Teen Over-The-Counter (OTC) and Prescription (Rx) Drug Use Stats

The reports are in: Although the percentage of teens using illegal drugs is down, the number of teens abusing prescription medication and OTC drugs has reached record highs.

Drugs such as OxyContin, Ritalin, and Vicodin have become so common among today's youth that more than 15% of high school seniors say they have taken at least one prescription or OTC pill for non-medical purposes within the past twelve months. And in 2005, the National Survey on Drug Use and Health revealed that more than 2 million teens had abused prescription drugs that year alone. [22]

Generation Rx

Today teenagers are not using as much cocaine, crack, LSD, and ecstasy as the teenagers of the 1960s. Kids have found other ways and means to get high—painkillers and other prescription drugs are being abused at record levels. This up coming generation of teens has been given the name "Generation Rx."

Teens are often getting caught raiding their parent's or grandparent's medicine cabinet in order to get high. For the first time, national studies show that today's teens are more likely to have abused a prescription painkiller than any illicit drug.[23]

Teen Marijuana Stats

Marijuana is the most widely used illicit drug used by teens today. Approximately 60% of the kids who use drugs use only marijuana. Of the 14.6 million marijuana users in 2002, approximately 4.8 million used it on 20 or more days in any given month.

The marijuana that is available to teens today is much stronger than the marijuana that was available in the 1960s. Sometimes it is also laced with other, more potent drugs. Marijuana is physically addictive. Each year, 100,000 teens are treated for marijuana dependence. Teens who smoke marijuana heavily experience much the same symptoms of withdrawal as users of nicotine.[24]

Marijuana

Regular marijuana users often develop breathing problems, such as chronic coughing and wheezing. Marijuana contains the same cancer causing chemicals as tobacco. The amount of tar inhaled by marijuana smokers and the level of carbon monoxide absorbed by those who smoke marijuana are three to five times greater than among tobacco smokers.[25]

Teen Drug and Alcohol Stats

Reported Drug and Alcohol Use by High School Seniors, 2007

	Used Within the Last:	
Drugs	12 Months*	30 Days
Alcohol	66.4%	44.4%
Marijuana	31.7%	18.8%
Other Opiates	9.2%	3.8%
Stimulants	7.5%	3.7%
Sedatives	6.2%	2.7%
Tranquilizers	6.2%	2.6%
Cocaine	5.2%	2.0%
Hallucinogens	5.4%	1.7%
Inhalants	3.7%	1.2%
Steroids	1.4%	1.0%
Heroin	0.9%	0.4%[26]

*Including the last month. Source: Press release: *Overall, Illicit Drug Use by American Teens Continues Gradual Decline in 2007*, University of Michigan News and Information Services, December 11, 2007.

Chapter Twelve
DRIVING UNDER THE INFLUENCE

● ● ● ● ● ● ● ●

Driving Under the Influence

You should never drink if you plan to drive. Always arrange to have a designated driver that will not drink if you will be somewhere alcohol is served.

If Stopped by the Police

If you are stopped for driving under the influence (DUI), expect the police to ask you:
- What you had to drink
- What drugs you may have taken

The police officer will ask you to give a breath and/or blood sample to test for drugs or alcohol.

By using a public road, it is automatically assumed in almost all states that you have provided your implied consent to such tests and samples.

Criminal Offense

In some states if you refuse to take a breath or blood test for the first time it is a civil violation—after that, it is a criminal offense.

Busted

An Aberdeen teen was arrested twice in one day on drunken driving charges—once as a 17-year-old and once as an 18-year-old.

Here's how it happened.

Montesano police arrested 17-year-old driver Domingo Ramos-Garcia yesterday afternoon and took him to the Grays Harbor County Jail (WA) for a breath test. Because he was 17, he was released to his father.

Five hours later he was arrested again on Highway 12 near Montesano by the same deputy who had dealt with him earlier.

But he wasn't booked until after midnight—after he turned 18.

As an adult, he was jailed.

Undersheriff Rick Scott says the teen also was arrested (previously) for driving under the influence.[1]

Busted

Drinking and driving kills.

Police arrested 19-year-old Katie Amanda McKewon on Wednesday on suspicion of gross vehicular manslaughter while intoxicated and felony drunken driving in connection with a fatal collision on Foothill Road on October 20.

Toxicology reports determined McKewon's blood alcohol level was three time the legal limit of 0.08 for drivers 21 and older.

It is illegal for anyone younger than 21 to be driving with any measurable alcohol in their system.

Her passenger, 19-year-old Laurel Williams, was killed in the crash.

Officer Bob Leong said the police investigation of the crash revealed that McKewon and Williams had attended an all-night party where alcohol was served.

Several "persons of interest" have been identified who investigators believe purchased and distributed the alcohol.

"We just want to re-emphasize that the girls were 19 years old," Leong said. "they should not have been drinking. Teenagers, just by their nature, have not driven a lot, and they are not good at it. Adding alcohol into that is not a good mix."[2]

Mode of Transportation

In most areas, drunk driving applies not only to all motorized vehicles but it also includes boats, golf carts, snowmobiles, motorcycles, mopeds, bulldozers, forklifts, and even Zamboni's. In fact, on some college campuses such as the University of California Santa Barbara, where there are thousand of bikes and bicycle lanes throughout the campus, you can receive a BUI for bicycling under the influence.

Busted

Some people refuse to learn from their mistakes. Please note that this incident occurred prior to the zero tolerance laws noted below.

Morgan Hills driver arrested three times in just 11 days for Driving Under the Influence in California...

Over an eleven day period during a December DUI crackdown held by Santa Clara County law enforcement, Anthony Maher was arrested for driving under the influence three times.

At the first traffic stop, the 19-year-old man from Morgan Hill, California, registered a blood alcohol content of .08%, the legal limit for an adult. Police ticketed Maher and held him at a police station for a couple of hours. Though he was an underage DUI suspect, and thus subject to harsher penalties, Maher was released because he had no prior arrest record.

At Maher's second arrest his BAC was .20%, four times the legal limit for a teen. During his third arrest his BAC was .21%. In both cases, police held the suspect for a few hours and released him to an adult. There was an option of detaining Maher in jail, which police now admit they should have done.

There are no laws for addressing three DUI arrests in such a short period of time. Because Maher had not gone to trial, let alone been arraigned, in any of his cases, all three arrests were labeled misdemeanors and, as allowed by California DUI laws, he was given a 30 day temporary driver's license.

If convicted in all three cases, Maher could be required to pay huge fines, attend alcohol education classes, perform community service, pay high-risk auto insurance premiums, and serve time in jail. His license would be suspended for three years.[4]

Penalties for Drunk Driving

DUI's in most states can:
* Be a misdemeanor
* Result in jail time
* Subject you to a fine.

You can also be required to complete a drug and/or alcohol counseling program.[5]

In most states, a DUI arrest that you are convicted for may subject you to a mandatory fine and possible jail time, regardless of your blood alcohol level results.

Loss of Driver's License

In some states, you will also lose your driver's license for one year for a first DUI offense, three years for a second DUI offense, and ten years for a third offense.

Zero Tolerance

Every state now employs strict alcohol laws for teens under the term "Zero Tolerance." This means that it is illegal for any teen driver to operate a vehicle with any amount of alcohol in your system. Even if your blood alcohol count (BAC) registers 0.01, or if the arresting officer smells a whiff of alcohol on your breath, you will face a list of DUI penalties from fines to license suspension.

Busted

Passenger DUI—a novel yet logical arrest

A Pennsylvania man is fighting a DUI charge, on the grounds that he was in the passenger's seat.

A state trooper said Derek Pittman had reached over and was steering the car while the driver was taking a bite of a sandwich that he was holding in both hands.

The trooper said the car was weaving on the road before he pulled it over. He said he then noticed a strong odor of alcohol coming from the car and saw the driver holding a large sandwich with both hands. So he gave Pittman a field sobriety test and he failed.

The trooper said the alcohol odor wasn't coming from the driver; it was coming from Pittman. Records show that when the trooper asked the driver why the car was swerving, Pittman leaned across the front seat and told the trooper it was his fault because he had briefly held onto the steering wheel while his friend was taking a bite of his sandwich.

Pittman's attorney said the driver never took his hand off the steering wheel, so the charge could be thrown out.

Police said the driver passed a breath test, but the passenger had a blood-alcohol content nearly three times the legal limit for driving in Pennsylvania. The Associated Press earlier reported that the driver was not given a sobriety test, but later corrected that statement.[7]

Busted

Boating under the influence in Venice

A drunken Italian woman stole a water taxi and went joyriding through Venice, Italy.

The 20-year-old had been celebrating the end of the carnival period and police said she was "considerably under the influence."

She jumped into the unmanned motorboat and rammed a number of moored boats before getting into a wild chase through the complex canal network with Venetian water police.

The young woman, who was inexperienced on the water, was said to be driving so uncontrollably that by the end of the chase all four policemen were injured and "numerous other boats" were damaged.

According to local police, she has been arrested and charged with theft, property damage, bodily harm, and resisting arrest.[6]

Chapter Thirteen
STEROID USE

● ● ● ● ● ● ● ●

Steroid Use

You should stay away from steroids as the manufacture, delivery, use, and/or sale of anabolic steroids is unlawful, but more importantly, the harmful impact they have on your health, growth, and sexual performance is well documented.

In most states, punishment for use is a ninety (90) day misdemeanor and/or a $100 fine.

Selling steroids can result in up to a seven (7) year jail term and/or a $5,000 fine.[2]

Steroids, the popular name for synthetic substances related to the male sex hormones, promote muscle growth and the development of male sexual characteristics. Steroids are legally available only with a prescription. They are prescribed to treat conditions such as delayed puberty, some types of impotence, and body wasting in patients suffering from AIDS. Steroids are often used and abused to enhance athletic performance and to improve physical appearance. Individuals who abuse steroids may take doses that are 10 to 100 times higher than those used for medical conditions. The National Institute on Drug Abuse reports that estimates of the number of individuals 18 and older who abuse steroids is in the hundreds of thousands.

Busted

You should note that...

A fast growing way of getting busted for personal steroid use is by ordering them by mail.[1]

High School Use

Steroid abuse among high school students is a particular problem. Four percent of high school seniors in the United States abused steroids at least once in their lifetime...according to the University of Michigan's Monitoring the Future Survey.

Roid Rage

Emotional problems associated with steroid use include dramatic mood swings (including manic symptoms that can lead to violence called roid rage), depression, paranoid jealousy, extreme irritability, delusions, and impaired judgment.[3]

Dangers of Steroids

Anabolic steroids cause many different types of problems. Less serious side effects include acne, oily hair, purple or red spots on the body, swelling of the legs and feet, and persistent bad breath. A teen that takes steroids might not grow as tall as he or she was supposed to grow. Some other serious and long-lasting side effects are:
- Premature balding
- Dizziness
- Roid rage, mood swings, including anger and sadness
- Seeing or hearing things that aren't there (hallucinations)

Nasty Teens

Hamsters with roid rage reveal that human teens may stay nasty for more than two years, with possible long-term brain impact.

Anabolic steroids not only make teens more aggressive, but may keep them that way into young adulthood. The effect ultimately wears off, but there may be other, lasting consequences for the developing brain. These findings, published in the February 2006 issue of *Behavioral Neuroscience*, also showed that aggression rose and fell in synch with neurotransmitter levels in the brain's aggression control region.[4]

- Extreme feelings of mistrust or fear (paranoia)
- Problems sleeping
- Nausea
- Vomiting
- Trembling
- High blood pressure that can damage the heart or blood vessels over time
- Aching joints
- Greater chance of injuring muscles and tendons
- Jaundice or yellowing of the skin (liver damage)
- Trouble urinating
- Increased risk of developing heat disease and stroke
- Cancer
- Liver tumors
- Kidney tumors
- Fluid retention
- Severe acne
- Increased cholesterol

These risks affect females:
- Increased facial hair growth
- Deepening voice, like a man's
- Shrinking of the breasts
- Period changes
- Pattern baldness

Specific risks for males include:
- Shrinkage of the testicles
- Pain while urinating
- Breast development
- Reduced sperm count
- Infertility
- Baldness
- Increased risk of prostate problems

Risks for people still growing, include:
- Prematurely halting growth
- Acceleration of puberty[5]

In addition to the risks directly associated with steroid abuse, individuals who inject the drugs expose themselves to risk of needle-borne diseases, including HIV (human immunodeficiency virus), hepatitis B and C, and other blood-borne viruses.

Street Names

Street terms for steroids include:
- Arnolds
- Gym Candy
- Juice
- Pumpers
- Stackers
- Weight Trainers[6]

Chapter Fourteen
CONTRACTS

● ● ● ● ● ● ● ●

Contracts

Once you turn 18, you can enter into legal agreements and contracts. A contract is an enforceable, whether written or oral, agreement between two or more parties that creates an obligation to do or not do a particular thing.

You should know that not all contracts must be in writing. But, any agreement involving real estate, that will last more than one year, or is for payment of someone else's debt must be in writing to be enforceable.

Understand the Contract

Do not sign an agreement that you do not understand. If you do not understand what you must sign, ask for someone to explain it to you or have a lawyer review it for you.

- Do not sign an agreement without reading it first.
- If you do not understand every provision of the agreement, have a lawyer review it before you sign it.
- If any provision is not as you agreed to, cross it out and initial your cross-outs.
- Write in any required corrections to the agreement and initial your corrections.
- Never sign an agreement that contains spaces that are blank.
- **Make certain that all parties to the agreement sign it.**
- **Get a copy of the fully executed (signed) agreement.**
- You should never accept the other parties' assurance or explanation of the meaning of any section of the contract. Get it verified, preferably by an attorney.
- **Once an agreement is put in writing and signed by the parties, and if a court is required to interpret and rule on the terms of the contract, the judge as a rule will not allow oral understandings (parol evidence) to be considered in the event there is a dispute over the terms and/or meaning of the agreement.**
- Do not waive any rights in the contract that you have as a matter of law.
- Do not waive any rights that you have in the agreement.
- Before you sign an agreement, make certain that you can meet all of the obligations agreed to by you. If you cannot, do not sign it.
- Do not agree to provisions that place unfair or unduly onerous penalties on you such as a confession of judgment.[2]

Common Contracts

Common agreements you will enter into after you turn 18 are:
- Sales contracts for products
- Sales contracts for services
- Credit card agreements
- Software licenses
- Leases on rental property
- Insurance policies
- Installment loan agreements (for computers, TVs, etc.)
- Car loans
- Student loans

Why a Contract Should Be Written

It is a good practice to put agreements in writing for the following reasons:

- To spell out clearly all of the terms of agreement between the parties.
- To reduce misunderstandings and disagreements if the oral agreement is unclear.
- To spell out clearly the parties' responsibilities.
- To help resolve disputes that may arise.
- The agreement should be clear and unambiguous so that any person that reads it will know the intent of the parties.[1]

Confession of Judgment

In contract law, confession of judgment refers to a type of contract (or a clause with such a provision) in which a party agrees to let the other party enter a judgment against him or her. Such contracts are highly controversial and may be invalidated as a violation of due process by courts, since you are essentially contracting away your right to raise any legitimate defenses in advance.

A typical confession of judgment is: "The undersigned irrevocably authorizes any attorney to appear in any court of competent jurisdiction and confess a judgment without process in favor of the creditor for such amount as may then appear unpaid hereon and to consent to immediate execution upon such judgment." Be on the lookout for these type of onerous provisions and do not accept them.

Breach of Contract

If you fail to perform your agreement with another party, it is called a breach of agreement. If you breach a contract:

- You may be liable for all the damages (losses) that the other party incurs owing to your breach.
- The other party can sue you in court to collect what is owed.
- The other party (in some instances) can ask the court to force you to perform your obligations under the contract (specific performance).
- If you agreed to pay for goods such as a car, the other party may repossess it. If repossessed, you may incur collection charges and related costs, as well as still be required to pay some of your debt.[3]

Garnishment

As additional remedies for your breach of a contract, a judge may have your paycheck or bank account garnished. This means a certain dollar amount will be deducted automatically from your paycheck or bank account until the judgment is paid in full.

- In other instances, the court can order that your personal property be sold publicly by the sheriff to satisfy your judgment.
- The enforceability of provisions in contracts can depend upon whether they are considered material violations of the agreement (important or substantial) or immaterial ones.

Warranties

When you make a major purchase, the manufacturer or seller makes an important promise to stand behind the product. This is called a warranty. Federal law requires that warranties be available for you to read before you buy an item, even when you are shopping by catalog or on the Internet. Warranty coverage varies, so you can compare the warranty coverage among manufacturers or sellers the same as you compare the style, price, and other characteristics of products.

The Magnuson-Moss Warranty Act was passed to regulate the control and impact of warranties for consumer products. This law also distinguishes between full and limited warranties.

Full Warranties

If you receive a full warranty with your purchase, the manufacturer or dealer is entitled to a reasonable amount of opportunities to fix the problems with the product you purchased. If not, you must be allowed to select either a replacement product without charge or a full refund.

The full warranty is enforceable by anyone who owns the product during the warranty period.

Limited Warranties

As the word implies, your remedies are significantly reduced with a limited warranty. You will not have the option to request a replacement product or full refund under a limited warranty.

Warranties: Preventing Problems

To minimize your problems when making purchases:

- **Read the warranty before you buy a product.** When online, look for hyperlinks to the full warranty or to an address where you can write to get a free copy. Understand exactly what protection the warranty gives you. If a copy of the warranty is available when shopping online, print it out when you make your purchase and keep it with your records.
- **Consider the reputation of the company offering the warranty.** Look for an address to write to or a phone number to call if you have questions or problems. If you are not familiar with the company, ask your local or state consumer protection office or Better Business Bureau if they have any complaints against the company. A warranty is only as good as the company that stands behind it.
- **Save your receipt and file it with the warranty.** You may need it to document the date of your purchase or prove that you are the original owner in the case of a nontransferable warranty.
- **Perform required maintenance and inspections so as not to void the warranty.**
- **Use the product according to the manufacturer's instructions.** Abuse or misuse may void your warranty coverage.[4]

Oral Warranties

If a salesperson makes a promise orally, e.g., the company will provide free repairs, get it in writing. Otherwise, you may not be able to get the service that was promised.[5]

Implied Warranties

Implied warranties are created by state law, and all states have them. Almost every purchase you make is covered by an implied warranty.

The most common type of implied warranty—a warranty of merchantability—means that the seller promises that the product will do what it is supposed to do. For example, a car will run and a toaster will toast.

Another type of implied warranty is the warranty of fitness for a particular purpose. This applies when you buy a product on the seller's advice that it is suitable for a particular use. For example, a person who suggests that you buy a certain sleeping bag for zero-degree weather warrants that the sleeping bag will be suitable for zero degrees.

If your purchase does not come with a written warranty, it is still covered by implied warranties unless the product is marked "as is," or the seller otherwise indicates in writing that no warranty is given. However, several states, including Kansas, Maine, Maryland, Massachusetts, Mississippi, Vermont, West Virginia, and the District of Columbia, do not currently permit "as is" sales.

If problems arise that are not covered by a written warranty, look to see if you have any protection in an implied warranty.

Implied warranty coverage can last as long as four years, although the length of the coverage varies from state to state.[6]

False Advertising

By general business law in most states, any advertising which is misleading in any material respect (significant) is considered to be false advertising.

An advertisement is considered misleading if it fails to disclose facts which are important in light of what is stated in the advertisement or facts which are relevant in the light of the customary use of the product.

"Free"

The Federal Trade Commission governs how the word "free" or similar words such as "bonus" and "gift" can be used in ads.

If you must do something or buy something in order to get a "free" item, certain conditions must be clearly disclosed.

Consumer Protection Laws

At 18, since you can enter into a contract in your own name, you should be aware of the following consumer-related laws:

Door-to-Door Sales: The Federal Trade Commission regulations give you three (3) days to cancel any credit contract or cash deal over $25.00 in value if the sales takes place away from the seller's regular place of business—for example, at your apartment door.

Credit Cards: Credit card companies are not allowed to send credit cards to you that you did not request. The law also limits your liability if an unauthorized person uses your credit card.

Truth-In-Lending: This law requires lenders to disclose specific contract provisions and credit costs to you.

Fair Credit Reporting: Under this law, credit reporting agencies must obtain certification from people who use credit reports, provide consumers access to credit reports, provide consumers with the right to dispute information contained in the records, and re-investigate any disputed information upon the consumer's request. Credit-granting organizations are required to disclose the reasons for denial of credit.

Motor Vehicles: For the purchase of cars, this law sets forth the provisions that must be in any financing agreement used to buy a car:
- The finance agreement must contain the amount of the finance charge
- The Finance Agreement must contain any other charges you must pay beyond the purchase price of the car.[7]

How To Avoid Phone Scams

- Say "no" and hang up when being hounded by high-pressure tactics!
- Be wary of advertisements that give little or no information other than a toll free number.
- Do not give your credit card number over the phone unless you know the company.[8]

Watch Out for These High Pressure Sales Tactics

- A demand for an immediate decision. These salespeople want you to make a quick decision before you have any second thoughts or consult a professional.
- A reluctance to provide information about the sales firm or the investment.
- Comments by salespeople about "inside information" or "secret" technology. They also may claim that celebrities, major corporations, or banks will be investing shortly.
- Delayed delivery of the product and/or investment profits. Beware of promises involving delays of more than a few weeks for delivery of your product or investment.
- Unusual arrangement for collecting funds from consumers, such as using an overnight courier or sending a courier or cab to pick up the check. This is how some con artists avoid mail fraud charges.[9]

Chapter Fifteen
EMPLOYMENT

• • • • • • • • •

Employment

Contract

Once you turn 18, you are able to work most jobs. However, most employers in the United States do not provide employees with written employment agreements. A written contract can establish limits on the ability of your employer to fire you.

Employee-At-Will

If you do not have a written agreement, you can be fired at any time for any reason or no reason, without advance notice. Without an employment agreement, you are called an employee-at-will. In most jobs in the United States, you will be an employee-at-will.

Questions Employers Should Not Ask

Federal and state laws prohibit prospective employers from asking certain questions that are not related to the job they are hiring for. Questions should be job-related and not used to find out personal information.

Employers should not ask about any of the following, because to not hire a candidate because of any one of them is discriminatory:
- Race
- Birthplace
- Color
- Sex
- Religion
- Birthplace
- Age
- Disability
- Marital/family status[1]

Complaint

If you believe you have been discriminated against, you should contact your state Department of Human Rights or similar agency. In California, for example, it is the Department of Employment and Fair Housing. You can also contact an attorney specializing in employment law.

Sick and Vacation Days

Your employer only has to provide you with sick and/or vacation leave as specified in a contract between you and the employer, or as may be set forth in a collective (labor) bargaining agreement.

Discrimination

You cannot be fired or discriminated against by your employer based on your:
- Age
- Race
- Color
- Disability
- Sex
- Religion
- Or because you filed a complaint against your employer to a government agency

Failure to Pay

If your employer fails to pay you, you can file a wage claim against the employer with your state Department of Labor.

Work Permits

Generally, if you are 18 or over or a high school graduate (or the equivalent), you do not need a work permit to start a job.[2]

Minimum Wage

In most jobs, your employer is required to pay you the higher of the federal law minimum hourly wage rate or your state's minimum per hour wage rate.

Minimum Wage

A minimum wage is the lowest hourly, daily, or monthly wage set by your state that employers may legally pay to employees or workers.

All states have a 40-hour work week with the exception of Kansas and Minnesota, where it is 46 and 48, respectively. If you work this many hours each week, you must be paid the minimum hourly rate mandated by your state.[3]

Exceptions

Certain administrative and professional jobs that pay a commission (such as for sales) do not have to pay the minimum wage rate. But, if your commissions when totaled are less than you would have earned under the minimum wage, your boss is required to make up the difference. [4]

Tips

If you primarily work for tips (valet, waiter, etc.), the minimum wage may not apply.[5]

Some states allow employers to count tips given to their workers as credit towards the minimum wage level.[7]

Online Posting Dangers

Do not post anything online that you would not want a prospective employer to see. Many employers now routinely check MySpace, Facebook, and other popular social networking sites for information about you that you would not reveal during a job interview or in a written job application.

Fair Labor Standards Act

The Fair Labor Standards Act (FLSA) establishes the minimum wage, overtime pay, record-keeping, and child labor standards affecting full-time and part-time workers in the private sector and in federal, state, and local governments. Covered, non-exempt workers are entitled to the minimum wage per hour. Overtime pay at a rate of not less than one and one-half times their regular rates of pay is required after forty (40) hours of work in a work week.

Overtime

You are not entitled to overtime pay until you work more than forty (40) hours per week (46 hours in Kansas and 48 hours in Minnesota). Those under 18 cannot earn overtime—it is a violation of the child labor laws for a minor to work greater than forty (40) hours a week.

Busted

Be careful what you post on Facebook, MySpace, or other social media sites.

An employer who was ready to hire a student from Vermont Technical College in Randolph Center changed his mind after seeing the student's Facebook page, says Lauri Sybel, director of the college career center. Since then, Sybel says she has checked other students' pages to make sure they weren't hurting their job prospects.[6]

Overtime Pay

An employer who requires or permits you to work overtime is generally required to pay you premium pay for such overtime work.[8]

Requirements

Unless specifically exempted, employees covered by the FLSA must receive overtime pay for hours worked in excess of 40 in a workweek at a rate not less than time and one-half their regular rates of pay. There is no limit in the FLSA on the number of hours employees aged 16 and older may work in any workweek. The FLSA does not require overtime pay for work on Saturdays, Sundays, holidays, or regular days of rest.

The overtime requirement may not be waived by agreement between the employer and employees. An agreement that only 8 hours a day or only 40 hours a week will be counted as working time also fails the test of FLSA compliance. An announcement by the employer that no overtime work will be permitted, or that overtime work will not be paid for unless authorized in advance, also will not impair your right to be paid for overtime that is worked.[9]

Pay Raises

Pay raises are generally a matter of agreement between you an your employer. Extra pay for working weekends or nights is also a matter of agreement between the employer and you, as well as for vacation pay, sick and holiday pay, severance pay, and performance evaluation pay.

Employment Agencies

A potential resource to help you locate a job is an employment agency. Usually the agencies must be state licensed. Some states limit the fee they can charge you to find a job to one week of your annual salary. However, the fee for an employment agency is ordinarily paid by the employer seeking an employee.[10]

Fee Recovery

In some instances, if you do pay a fee and your job lasts less than one month, you may be able to recover some or all of the employment agency fee you paid.

If You Lose Your Job

If you lose your job, obviously a major issue you must deal with is providing for yourself and your family. Finding out if you qualify for unemployment compensation should be the first thing you take care of. The next thing is applying for this benefit. There are certain criteria that must be met. In the United States, your local Employment Service Center will be able to help you. The U.S. Department of Labor website (www.dol.gov) has information on unemployment compensation in the United States, including links to the individual sites for many states.

The next issue to deal with is health insurance. In the United States the majority of people who have health insurance are covered under a group plan through their employer. When a job is lost, that coverage is as well. That is why The Consolidated Omnibus Budget Reconciliation Act (COBRA) was passed some time ago. This law allows those separated from their jobs to purchase health insurance at a group rate for a limited time.[11]

Worker's Compensation

The Workers' Compensation Law entitles you to compensation payments if you are not able to work owing to work-related injuries. You are also entitled to payments for medical expenses related to your injuries.

Only Remedy

In most cases, workers' compensation is your exclusive remedy against your employer if you are injured on the job. This means that you cannot sue your employer or co-worker for getting injured at work.

If You Are Injured on the Job

Before receiving medical treatment, you have the responsibility to tell the doctor how you were injured and if you believe the injury may be work-related, and whether it may be a worker compensation-related injury. The insurance company has the right to terminate benefits on your claim until the workers compensation board reviews your claim and makes a temporary decision based on the facts.[12]

Drug Testing in the Workplace

Most states permit some form of drug testing in the workplace. In these states, employers may legally ask you to take a blood test or provide a urine sample for any reason or no reason at all. Employers do not need a warrant or even probable cause. Employers may randomly drug test you on any reasonable basis they establish.

Professional Counseling

In some states, companies with more than twenty (20) employees must make professional counseling available to all employees that test positive for drug use and want to keep their jobs while receiving counseling.

Your employer can suspend you with full pay pending the results of your drug test.

If you test positive, an employer may:
- Fire you
- Not hire you
- Discipline you
- Move you to another job

You do not have to take a drug test, but if you refuse you may get terminated.[14]

Failing a Drug Test

Owing to the great controversy over invasion of privacy and the accuracy of drug testing, you are not likely to be arrested for failing a workplace drug test.[15]

Income Taxes

Regardless of your age, when you work you are required by law to pay income taxes on the pay that you receive if you have gross income of more than $2,550 for a tax year. This applies to federal income taxes and state income taxes.

You are required to file a federal income tax return and your state income tax return on or before April 15th of each year for the taxes due for the preceding calendar year.

Your employer should withhold these taxes from your pay to cover your taxes.[16]

Workplace Violence

Working alone is a major risk factor associated with violence in the workplace.

Also, working late night or early morning hours constitutes a hazard. Statistics indicate that fewer customers and the potential for more cash on hand make retail environments prime targets during these hours.

High crime areas obviously pose a threat.

To ensure a safe workplace, contact the local police to determine if the business is in a high crime area or if crimes have been committed in the past. Talk to others who work for the business to determine the potential for problems of violence or gang-related activity.

At the job interview, ask questions related to security and the safety measures taken to protect employees.

Talk to the supervisor to ensure he or she is aware of teen concerns and that satisfactory action to address safety issues will be taken.

Questions to ask about workplace safety and security:
- Does the business visibly post statements about the amounts of cash on hand?
- Is lighting adequate both inside and outside at entrances and exits and in the parking lot and garbage disposal areas?
- Is there a working alarm system?
- Are video cameras or mirrors used to deter crime?
- Is a buddy system in place with a neighboring business in the event of an unforeseen action?
- Is a system set up with local security and police patrols?
- Is more than one person on premises to open and close?
- Are employees trained in case someone suspicious approaches them or attempts a robbery?
- Has a security survey of the business been conducted?[18]

• • • • • • • •

Chapter Sixteen
AUTOMOBILES

• • • • • • • •

Buying a Car

As you are likely to buy a car once you turn 18 years of age, you should be familiar with what to be on the lookout for before you shop for a car. A car is likely to be the second largest purchase you will make in your lifetime, following the purchase of a home, so you should be well prepared before you go car shopping.

Buying Used

The Federal Trade Commission's (FTC) Used Car Rules requires dealers (someone who sells six [6] or more cars a year) to post a Buyer's Guide in every used car they offer for sale.

Buyer's Guide

The Buyer's Guide must tell you:
- Whether the vehicle is being sold "as is" or with a warranty
- What percentage of the repair costs a dealer will pay under the warranty
- That spoken promises are difficult to enforce
- To get all promises in writing
- To keep the Buyer's Guide for reference after the sale
- The major mechanical and electrical systems on the car, including some of the major problems you should look out for
- To ask to have the car inspected by an independent mechanic before you buy.[1]

Car Inspection

You should always have any used car you desire to purchase inspected and evaluated by a trusted independent mechanic. If the seller will not provide you with that opportunity, you should find another car to buy from a different seller.

Be Practical

When buying a car, think beyond the superficial and emotional. Consider:
- Gas mileage
- Safety
- Collision rating
- Reliability
- Service records
- Cost to insure

Buying a Used Car

As few 18-year-olds purchase a new car, at a minimum, you should do the following before you buy a used car:
- Check its past service history
- Find out if it was involved in a major accident (also check www.carfax.com)
- Have a mechanic check the cars' frame and engine
- Determine its accurate mileage
- Make sure it has a proper title
- Take it for a test drive on city streets and on a highway.

Required Used Car Data

In most states, a used car must have the following information on a window sticker:
- Make of the car
- Model name
- Year of manufacture
- Serial number
- Name and address of previous owner(s) (you should ask for this information)
- It should also state if the odometer was ever repaired or replaced and the actual mileage that has been driven on the car
- How the car was previously used by its owner (e.g. police car, limo, taxi, rental, personal use, etc.)
- How the dealer obtained the car (e.g. auction, repossession, trade-in, etc.)
- Any major accidents
- Any known defects that the dealer is aware of
- Any significant damage to the car by collision, water, or fire as known by the dealer
- Whether the care is sold "as is" or has any implied warranties (Please see page 99)
- A written policy concerning the dealer's practices on returning your deposit
- Also, find out if the car was returned to the dealer under a Lemon Law.[2]

Gather Information

If the sticker on the windshield does not have enough information, ask for more information. If you can, call the previous owner to find out what you can about the car, especially why it was sold.

Take a Road Test

Always take the car you would like to buy on a test drive. This is a good opportunity for you to really check the car out before you make a decision to buy it.

Before you get into the vehicle, check the following:
- Are the tires in safe condition—no cracks, splits, or excessive wear?
- Is the car in overall good condition?
- Are the seats, carpets, switches, mirrors, etc. all in acceptable shape?
- Is the seat comfortable, evenly padded, in good repair, and adjustable?
- Do the safety features work—horn, headlights, emergency brake, seatbelts, and windshield wipers?

Before you go for a test drive, check the following:
- Is the car easy to start?
- Are the gears (manual transmission) easy to shift?
- Is the clutch easy to engage with no abnormal sounds or hesitation?
- In an automatic transmission, does the car move smoothly from gear to gear?
- Is there any unusual noise or hesitation while changing gears?
- Are the brakes strong?
- Is there a pull to either side as you step on the brakes?
- On the freeway, does the car have good acceleration?
- Can it easily reach speeds in order to merge with the flow of traffic?
- Do the turn signals work?
- Around town, does the car handle well and idle steadily during stops?
- Is the acceleration strong when starting off at a green light?
- Do the air conditioning and heating systems function properly?
- Does the wind whistle through windows that cannot quite close all the way?
- Check the sound system, if that is an important feature to you:
- Is the radio reception clear?
- Is the CD or DVD player functional? (You may want to bring one along just for a test.)

Under the Hood

Check to see if there is any dripping fluid, smoke billowing from the exhaust system, or any build up of dirt and grime on and around the engine. Ask to see the maintenance records and any receipts of auto parts and repairs for the car. Ask how long they have owned the vehicle. If they have not owned it very long, request the previous owner's name and phone number and give them a call. There may be real reasons why the latest owner is disappointed with the car and wanting to sell it right away.

Average Mileage

On average, cars are driven from 12,000 to 15,000 miles per year. If the car has significantly lower mileage, you should determine whether the seller may have improperly adjusted the odometer.

To Determine Mileage

You can determine the vehicles' accurate mileage by:
- Looking at the mileage noted on repair records
- Looking at the mileage noted on state inspection records
- Looking at the wear on the tires—if they are the original tires (most original tires last from 30,000 to 40,000 miles)
- Looking at the wear on the brake and gas pedals of the car
- Determine if the car has been repainted. If the miles are very low and it has been repainted, it may have been out of service owing to an accident.[3]

Totaled Car

In some states, if an insurance company has determined that a car has been totaled, this fact must be disclosed to the buyer by the seller orally and in writing.

Have a mechanic determine if the cars' frame has been damaged; if so, do not purchase that car. A damaged frame means the vehicle was involved in a fairly violent collision and its basic performance has probably been severely compromised.

Car History

Before you purchase a used car, check its history via Carfax (www.carfax.com). You can also ask the car dealer to supply a Carfax report for the car you are interested in buying. With this service you can find out:
- If the car has been totaled in an accident
- If the car has been salvaged
- Its "lemon" history
- Its title status
- State emission inspection results
- Lien activity
- Vehicle use (taxi, rental, lease, etc.)
- Service and repair history.

You will need the car's Vehicle Identification Number (VIN) to conduct this search. This number is usually inside the car's windshield at the very bottom on the driver's side.

Kelley Blue Book

You can now research the manufacturer's price for the car and options you want on www.kbb.com and other similar websites. It is easier to negotiate the purchase of a car, especially a new one, once you know the car dealer's price.

Other good sources of a car's value are:
- www.nadaguides.com
- www.edmunds.com

Finance Options

If you buy a car on credit, check the current credit alternatives from several sources, such as:
- The dealer (this is often a big moneymaker for the dealer, so watch out)
- Your bank (only if its rates are competitive)
- Your credit union
- Family
- Friends
- An independent car loan agency (make sure its rates are competitive)

Car Payment Options

When you buy a car you can pay the purchase price in full or you can finance the price over time. When you finance, the total cost of the car will increase as you are paying:
- The cost of credit
- Interest
- Other loan and processing costs

So, factor all of these costs in your purchase decision.

Car Loans

Do your homework and search for the lowest possible credit arrangement.

Bizarre Driving Laws: California

- Any woman dressed in a house coat is prohibited from driving a car.
- It is illegal in San Francisco to buff or dry your car with used underwear.
- No unoccupied vehicle may exceed 60 miles per hour.[4]

Car Finance

If you finance your car purchase, be certain you understand the following factors of your loan agreement:
- The exact price you are paying for your car
- The total amount you are financing
- The finance charge (what the credit will cost)
- The APR (the cost of credit each year)
- The number of payments
- The amount of payments
- The total sales price (the sum of the monthly payments plus the down payment)[5]

Car Loan of 48 Months

According to financial experts, if you cannot squeeze that car loan into 48 months, do not buy that car—you are heading down a path of destruction.

You don't want to spend the next 6 years paying off a car. Go buy a cheaper car instead. Remember, your car loan is but one of many cost items contributing to your overall cost of vehicle ownership. Most people overlook all the other cost items and get into trouble real quick, not realizing insurance goes up on a new car. You should create a budget that accounts for all your annual costs to own that car, like loan payments, tires, insurance, maintenance, etc. Then, from your budget, you should determine if you can handle that much of an annual drain on your finances. If you cannot afford a new car, buy a dependable used car like a Honda Accord or a Toyota Camry, which typically run years with out costly repair issues. That is what is most important with your first car, safety and dependability, especially once you head off to college and cannot afford a single thing to go wrong.[6]

Cooling Off Period

Dealers are not required by law to give used car buyers a three-day right to cancel. The right to return the car in a few days for a refund exists only if the dealer grants this privilege to buyers. Dealers also call this right to cancel:

- A cooling off period
- A money-back guarantee
- A no-questions-asked return policy

Bizarre Driving Laws: Georgia

- State Assembly members are immune from being ticketed for speeding while the State Assembly is in session.
- In Marietta, Georgia, it is illegal to spit from a moving car or bus, but it is okay from a moving truck.[7]

Car Repairs

In many states, no work on your car can be performed at a car repair shop until you receive a written estimate and authorize the repairs by signing the estimate or work order.

Always obtain a written estimate before you consent to any work being performed on your car. This estimate should include:

- Total estimated price for parts
- Total estimated price for labor
- A list of the parts to be used
- The method of repair

If additional work is then required, it cannot be done until the repair shop contacts you and obtains your consent.[8]

Return of Old Parts

At the time you sign the written estimate or work order, you may request that the shop return to you any parts that are replaced. You have to request the return of parts before the work is done. This is a good way to keep the repair shop honest, so they cannot say that a part has been replaced without doing so.[9]

Car Repair Rights

You have certain basic legal rights in most states when your car needs to be repaired:

- The repair shop must post its hourly rates for labor, or whether it charges set rates for certain services.
- You have a right to know which repair method will be used.
- You have a right to obtain a written estimate of the repair costs.
- You can set a written limit on the cost of the repairs that cannot be exceeded without your consent. If your consent is exceeded, you are not required to pay for the extra charges.
- You have a right to inspect all replaced parts unless the part has to be returned to the manufacturer under a warranty obligation.
- You have the right to know whether the parts that are being installed are new, used, or refurbished.[10] At times it may be much more economical for you to replace parts with rebuilt ones. You should evaluate this option on a case by case basis.

Rebuilt

A repair shop cannot use a refurbished or reconditioned part without your permission.

Car Repair Scams

Auto repair problems make up the largest group of consumer complaints. The National Highway Traffic Safety Administration estimates that consumers lose tens of billions of dollars each year owing to faulty or unnecessary car repairs. While most repair shops are honest, undercover car repair stings find dishonest auto mechanics and shops in most areas of the country.[11]

The Most Common Auto Repair Scams

Highway Bandits: This is one of the oldest auto repair scams in existence. These highway bandits own, or work for service stations. They prey on motorists who stop for gasoline, air, or water. They use numerous ploys. They have been known to spray oil or drip it under a vehicle, then claim that it leaked from the traveler's car. They have punctured tires, cut water hoses, and fan belts so that the motorist will have to buy new ones. These bandits focus on the danger the traveler faces if they drive off without making the repairs, and often charge inflated prices.

Maintenance Hook Schemes: Repair shops will advertise check-ups or preventive maintenance service at very reasonable rates. Unethical shops will use these maintenance specials to hook and deceive their customers. A simple oil change and lubrication process can turn into expensive and unneeded repairs. Some mechanics will even cause damage during an inspection to enhance their income by "discovering" new repair needs.

Part Replacement Problems: A lot of dishonest mechanics have charged customers for parts that were not used. In addition, the mechanic will charge you for the labor required to install the non-existent replacement. It is a double rip-off! Used parts are a viable option for many repairs, however, some mechanics charge customers for new, premium parts after installing sub-standard or used car parts. Always ask for your old, damaged parts back after it has been replaced. It helps keep your mechanic honest.

Counterfeit Car Parts: To save money, some unscrupulous repair shop owners cut costs by using counterfeit car parts instead of high-quality replacement parts. The difference in price can be significant but you will not see any of the savings. You will be billed the full price for the parts and will not be told. This practice can actually put you in danger because counterfeit auto parts are often of inferior quality. This can put you and your family at risk and you may never even know it. Besides being potentially unsafe, counterfeit parts generally wear out sooner than genuine parts. Detecting counterfeit auto parts is difficult because the counterfeiters often duplicate trademarks or alter them so slightly that it takes an experienced eye to notice the difference. If you suspect that counterfeit car parts have been used in place of quality materials, do not hesitate to file a report with your state's attorney general or local Better Business Bureau.[12]

113

State Auto Insurance Requirements

You must obtain automobile insurance for your car as mandated by the law in your state. There are websites such as www.personalinsure.com and www.about.com to find out the insurance requirements in your state.[13]

Factors That May Affect Your Insurance Premium

Rating factors are characteristics that place you in a group of drivers with similar risk-related characteristics. Companies set a rate for each group based on the claims paid for the people in that group. Here are some tips that may lower your insurance premiums:

- Keep a clean driving record. Drivers with accidents and tickets usually pay higher premiums than those with good driving records. For example, if you have more than one at-fault accident in less than three years, or if you are convicted of a moving violation, your insurance company could raise your premiums or non-renew your insurance policy. If your driver's license is suspended or revoked, your insurance company can cancel the policy. If you are under your parents' policy, your driving record will affect their insurance premium.
- Choose your vehicle carefully. Certain vehicles cost more to insure because they are more likely to be damaged in an accident, cost more to repair, or are frequently stolen. If you have a sports car or a high performance car you may have a hard time finding insurance at standard rates. And if your car is a "street machine" or is "souped-up" there is an even greater chance that you will pay a lot more for your insurance.
- Drive a vehicle with safety features. Some companies offer a discount for such items as air bags, automatic seatbelts, and anti-lock brakes.
- Maintain a good credit history. Companies may consider your financial stability and charge higher premiums based on your financial status (i.e., credit card history, amount of credit, how timely you pay your bills, etc.).
- Keep your grades up. Some companies offer a discount to young drivers who maintain a B average or better.[14]

Totaled Car

When an insurance company declares your car totaled after an accident, it is based on the value of your car and what it would cost to repair your car.

As a general practice, if the repair will exceed the value of the car, the insurance company will declare your car totaled and give you a cash settlement in lieu of paying for the repairs.

Independent Appraiser

If you disagree with the amount your insurance company is willing to pay you for your totaled car, you can bring in an independent appraiser to try to help you negotiate a higher settlement. You may have to pay for the appraiser, however.

Certificate of Inspection

In most states, the dealer is required to display a certificate of inspection that is issued no longer than sixty (60) days before the sale. Research the requirements in your state.

This inspection usually means that the following features on the vehicle work:
- Brakes
- Parking brake
- Lights
- Horn
- Windshield wipers
- Suspension
- Steering
- Exhaust system
- But not the engine (in many cases)

The car must also have:
- Tires with sufficient tread
- Correct alignment
- No rust holes in the car's body
- Rear view mirror
- Fenders
- Reflectors
- Windows that you can see through from inside and outside[15]

Unused Warranty Time

Some used cars still have some warranty time remaining from the previous owner that are permitted to be transferred to you. You should check with the dealer or the prior owner.[17] Also, it is useful to obtain all the paperwork and records the seller has concerning your car, especially as they relate to service records and warranties.

Failure to Pass Inspection

In some states, if the car you purchased does not pass inspection as promised by the Inspection Certificate, the car dealer must bring the car up to standard for free. If not, the dealer can be fined. [16]

Guide to Selling Your Car

Determine Your Asking Price

To sell your car, check comparable vehicles in classified ads or visit used car websites to determine the going rate for your make and model of car. Once you have a range of prices for your particular model and year of car, factor in a few other considerations:
- Mileage
- Condition
- Special features

Other factors that determine the selling price of a vehicle that some people do not consider are: location of the car (weather plays a big factor on the look and longevity of a vehicle), who has driven the car (young drivers are known to put hard miles on their cars), and gas mileage (this has become a major factor in deciding which car to buy).

If you have made major cosmetic or mechanical improvements to the car recently, increase your price accordingly. A new set of high quality tires, a rebuilt engine, a replaced transmission still under warranty, or a top-of-the-line paint job adds to the value of the car. Locate the paperwork regarding any major work and create a file of receipts (with dates) to show any potential buyers.

Once you have decided on what you plan to charge, raise your asking price by a few hundred dollars. That cushion will provide some room to negotiate with your potential buyers.

Decide Where to Sell

There are many methods to sell a used car, including hanging a "For Sale" sign in the vehicle, buying a classified ad in the local newspaper, posting a sign on neighborhood bulletin boards, and trading in the car at a nearby car dealership.

There are also Internet sites that will assist you in selling your vehicle. Many sites exist where buyers, usually for a small fee, can post their car's details and interested parties can contact you online for more information. Websites such as AutoTrader.com, Cash4UsedCars.com, CarSoup.com, CarsDirect.com, craigslist.com, FastAutoSales.com, and Yahoo.com can help streamline the sale of your car.

Detail Your Vehicle

Minor maintenance and clean-up will cost you little but enhance the appeal of your vehicle. Before selling consider the following improvements:
- Wash and wax the car
- Clean the interior and empty the trunk
- Clean the carpet and upholstery
- Shine the tires and hubcaps
- Make sure the tire pressure is at the recommended level
- Hang up an air freshener

Close the Deal

Only you can decide how payment will be made: by personal check, cash only, or cashier's check. It is always helpful to mention your payment preference while setting up an appointment to see the car. In that way, if the buyer wants your car on the spot, you will be able to finalize the transaction quickly. For safety, it is best for you to only accept cash or a bank check as payment.

Sign on the Dotted Line

Before undertaking the sale of any vehicle, get informed. Learn what your state's requirements are for such documents as title transfer, smog certification, and possibly an odometer reading statement prior to advertising your car for sale. [18]

Chapter Seventeen
RENTING PROPERTY

● ● ● ● ● ● ● ●

Your Rental Obligations

As a renter you are required to:
- Not disturb your neighbors' peaceful enjoyment of the premises
- Keep the premises clean
- Keep the premises safe
- Not deliberately or negligently damage, remove, or destroy any part of the premises, or knowingly permit a person to do so.

Renting

Many students rent property for the first time when they go away to college. Others do so when they opt for independent living from the family upon turning 18 or older. Therefore, you should be aware of the rules that both you and your landlord are required to follow in a rental arrangement.

When you rent an apartment or house you have to find out if the landlord wants you to sign a lease. If you are 18 or over you can now sign contractual documents such as a lease. Leases usually have a term of six (6) months or one (1) year.

If you have a signed lease, you cannot be asked to move out during its term unless you have failed to pay your rental obligations or violated a provision in the lease.

If you do sign a lease and move out before its term expires, you are contractually bound to pay the remaining months of rent due under the lease unless the landlord can mitigate his damages by finding someone else to move into the rental space.[1]

Roommate Moves Out

If you sign a lease with roommates and one of the roommates moves out, it is your responsibility to find another roommate or to make up the difference in each monthly rent payment.

Lease Terms

Your rental lease should include provisions for:
- Rent amount
- Length of the lease (term)
- Obligations of the landlord
- Obligations of the tenant

It's the Law: Maine

In Romford, Maine, it is illegal for a tenant to bite his/her landlord.[3]

There are certain terms that a rental lease should NOT include. Do not accept a rental lease that includes the following terms:

- Your agreement to waive any legal rights and remedies you have under the law
- You should never agree to indemnify (hold harmless) the landlord for any accidents or liabilities that occur on the property.
- You should never agree to a confession of judgment on any dispute arising out of your lease (please see page 98).
- You should never agree to pay for the landlord's legal fees.[2]

Landlord Obligations

Landlords are required to:

- Supply running water at all times
- Supply reasonable heat at all times
- Maintain the premises in a fit and safe manner
- Comply with housing codes affecting safety and health
- Maintain in safe working order the heating, plumbing, electricity, and other facilities supplied by the landlord
- Maintain the rental space in a fit and habitable condition
- Keep all common areas in a safe and clean condition

Rental Deposits

In most states the landlord can request a prepaid rental deposit that is not more than two (2) months of rent. This deposit will be applied against damage that you cause to the rental property or for unpaid rent at the termination of your lease.

Rental Deposits: Security

- As a general rule, you are not responsible for normal wear and tear of the apartment or home you rent.
- If you or your guests cause damage by carelessness or deliberate misuse, you must pay for it.[4]

Legitimate Deductions

Examples of items that can be deducted from your security deposit are:

- Cigarette burns
- Broken tiles
- Large marks or holes in the wall
- Door off of its hinges
- Rips in the carpet
- Pet stains
- Broken refrigerator shelf
- Picture holes in the wall that required patching and painting
- Water stains from plants
- Water stains from windows being left open
- Missing curtains/blinds
- Drains blocked by misuse

The landlord can withhold all or part of your deposit for:

- Past due rent
- Funds to repair damage you caused
- Expenses incurred by the landlord to enforce his rights under the lease

You are required to turn over the rental space in its original condition at the start of the leases (excluding normal wear and tear).

Tenant-At-Will

If you do not sign a lease, you automatically are considered a tenant-at-will or a month-to-month tenant. This means that you are only a tenant-at-will for thirty (30) day periods.

As a tenant-at-will, you can move out without penalties by providing thirty (30) days written notice to your landlord that you are leaving the apartment.

Of course, this also means that the landlord can ask you to leave by providing you with thirty (30) days written notice to do so. Without a written lease, no reason is required to ask you to vacate. If you do not leave after thirty (30) days notice the landlord can evict you.

Lawful Evictions

You can be lawfully evicted for the following reasons:

- **Non-payment of rent**: The landlord must inform the tenant in writing that full rent is due by a specific deadline or the lease will be terminated. If the landlord refuses to accept full payment and the tenant can prove it, the eviction can be challenged in court. After the deadline, the landlord does not have to accept payment.

- **Curable Rule Violations**: Some rental rules that are broken are curable (you have the opportunity to correct/fix the problem). These are:

  - Owning a pet in violation of a no-pet clause
  - Unauthorized guests
  - Not keeping the property sanitary
  - Moving in a roommate without notice
  - Failure to dispose of trash
  - Disturbing other tenants

- **Non-Curable Rule Violations:** These are:

  - Intentional misuse of the landlord's property
  - Intentional misuse of other tenants' property
  - Repeated, unreasonable disturbances
  - Violating criminal laws (if you are arrested or convicted)
  - Providing false information on your rental application
  - Making a false complaint concerning the safety or habitability of your space to a government agency.

- **Other tenant violations**: The landlord must inform the tenant in writing of the supposed violation. The tenant must have ample time to correct the problem. If the tenant does nothing to correct it, the landlord may evict.

In some states you can be evicted if:
- You do something that adversely and materially impacts the health and safety of others
- You physically assault or threaten another on the premises
- Your possess or illegally use firearms
- You possess controlled substances other than prescription drugs

- **Lease has expired:** If the landlord does not extend an expired lease and the tenant refuses to leave, the landlord may evict you.[5]

Eviction Process

To be evicted, your landlord must follow certain required steps and procedures:

- If you signed a lease, then you must have breached one of the terms of the lease.
- If you are a month-to-month tenant-at-will without a lease, or if your lease is a month-to-month time period, your landlord can evict you for any reason or no reason at all. However, the landlord cannot evict you in retaliation for you trying to enforce rights under the lease, such as requesting repairs be done.
- Before your landlord can evict you or file an eviction case in court, he must provide you with a Notice to Quit document.

Notice to Quit

A Notice to Quit is a written request from your landlord to you to move out or if you owe rent to move out and pay your overdue rent.

If you do not move out by the date indicated in the Notice to Quit, the landlord must then file an eviction case against you in court.

If you are evicted in the court proceeding you will usually have ten (10) days to leave your rental space.

If you fail to move out by the tenth day, the landlord can get a Court Order that will permit the sheriff to remove you and your property from the rental space on the tenth day.

If the eviction is because of failure to pay your rent, the judge may give you ten (10) days to move out or pay the rent that is past due.

Written Notice

To terminate your lease, your landlord must send you a written notice of your violation. The landlord must give you a reasonable period of time to fix the violation (if it is curable). A reasonable period is normally a week or two. If you do not fix the violation in a timely manner or move out, the landlord can start formal eviction proceedings.[6]

Illegal Eviction: Self Help

Landlords who take matters into their own hands often think that their behavior will be excused by the tenant's egregious conduct. However, the fact that the tenant did not pay rent, left the property a mess, verbally abused the manager, or otherwise acted outrageously will not be a valid defense—and, in fact, a landlord could end up on the wrong end of a lawsuit for trespass, assault, battery, slander or libel, intentional infliction of emotional distress, and wrongful eviction .

Shortcuts such as threats, intimidation, utility shut offs, or attempts to physically remove a tenant are illegal and dangerous. Virtually every state that forbids "self-help" evictions also imposes penalties for landlords who break the law. When tenants sue after being locked out, or frozen out, they cannot only sue for their actual money losses (such as the cost of temporary housing, the value of food that spoiled when the refrigerator stopped running, or the cost of an electric heater when the gas was shut off), but they can also sue for penalties, such as several month's rent. In some states, the tenant can collect and still remain in the premises; in others, tenants are entitled to monetary compensation only.[7]

Eviction: Withholding Rent

The law in most locations requires the tenant to inform the landlord in writing that he or she intends to withhold rent if a specific problem is not solved by a certain date. Tenants must give the landlord reasonable time to comply with their requests.

Illegal Evictions

In practically all jurisdictions, it is illegal for your landlord to:

- Turn off your heat, electricity, or other utilities, except for temporary interruptions for emergency repairs.
- Move your belongings out of your apartment without a court order unless you have abandoned the apartment.
- Padlock or change the lock on your door without a court order.
- Confiscate or deny you access to your belongings because of back rent or any other reason. If the landlord has lawfully removed your belongings, you can be required to pay the landlord for moving and storage charges.[8]

Late Rent

No Grace Period

Contrary to popular belief, you do not have a grace period to pay your rent late unless your written lease spells out a specified grace period.

If you do not have a grace period in your written lease, your landlord is free to terminate your tenancy with a pay or quit notice the day after your rent is due.

Constructive Eviction

When a landlord provides housing that is so substandard that a landlord has legally evicted the tenant, it is called constructive eviction. For example, if the landlord refuses to provide heat or water or refuses to clean up an environmental health hazard, the tenant may have the right to move out and stop paying rent, without incurring legal liability for breaking the lease.

Subletting

In most cases, you cannot sublet your apartment to another tenant without the landlord's written approval.

Rental Insurance

You may want to obtain renter's insurance or a tenant's homeowners insurance policy if you rent. This policy protects your property if you suffer a loss owing to:
- Theft
- Fire

It may also cover:
- Property damage
- Bodily injury damage
- Medical payments

If at College

A college students property located at school may be covered by your parent's homeowners insurance policy.

Moving Out

Before you move out of your rental space, give your new address in writing to the landlord so he/she knows where to return your deposit.

The landlord has thirty (30) days from the date you stopped renting, and the receipt of your new address, to return your deposit.

The landlord must give you a written explanation if all or part of your deposit is not being returned to you.

Insurance Discounts

Insurance companies frequently offer you a discount on your insurance coverage if you bundle your insurance with one company. Examples would be bundling your rental policy with your car insurance or an umbrella policy.

Chapter Eighteen
MARRIAGE

● ● ● ● ● ● ● ●

Marriage

Once you are 18, you no longer require the consent of your parents to marry. But, of course, you should not run out and do so without very careful thought and evaluation.

Marriage is defined as a lifelong legal contract between a man and a woman. Only the states of Connecticut, Iowa, Massachusetts, New Hampshire, Rhode Island, and Vermont currently allow same-sex marriage. States define what constitutes a marriage and the impact of divorce, dissolution, annulment, and marital problems.

Same Sex Marriage

Same sex marriage is also called:
- Gay marriage
- Equal marriage
- Gender-neutral marriage
- Lesbian marriage
- Homosexual marriage
- Single sex marriage
- Same gender marriage

Domestic Partners

Some states now recognize registered domestic partners for same-sex couples. Usually domestic partners are entitled to all of the rights, protection, and benefits that married couples receive. These benefits entitle you to:

- Healthcare coverage under each other's family benefits
- Adoption of each others' children
- Taking family leave of absence
- Obtaining property rights

Domestic Partnerships

Domestic partnerships, civil unions, or requested partnerships are allowed in California, Connecticut, Hawaii, Maine, New Hampshire, New Jersey, Oregon, Vermont, Washington (limited: one individual must be at least 62 years old), and the District of Columbia.

A domestic partnership is a legal or personal relationship between individuals who live together and share a common domestic life but are not joined in a traditional marriage or a civil union. It is also known as pairage.[1]

Valid Marriage

For a marriage to be legally valid, some of the requirements your state law may include are:

- Someone legally authorized to perform the marriage ceremony:
  - A judge
  - A clergy person
  - A justice of the peace
  - Others that are authorized to do so
- Mutual declarations from your spouse-to-be and you to "take" each other as "husband and wife"
- A competent adult witness (some states require two witnesses)
- A health certificate
- A certificate of registry of marriage
- A marriage license
- Both are 18 or have the consent of a parent or judge if younger

- Proof of immunity or vaccination for certain diseases
- Proof of termination of a prior marriage by death, judgment or dissolution (divorce), or annulment
- Sufficient mental capacity (ability to enter into a contract)
- The couple are not close blood relatives
- Satisfaction of a waiting period from the time the marriage license is issued until the marriage ceremony is performed
- Recording of the marriage license after the marriage ceremony is performed
- Consummation of the marriage by the act of sexual relations (only a few states require this)
- Some states require a blood test for venereal disease.

You should check the law in your particular state to find out the specific requirements for a valid marriage.

Do not get married until you can be certain that you can handle the emotional and financial expectations.

Busted

The lack of a minimum age for marriage in Kansas got a lot of attention recently with the case of Nebraskan Matthew Koso, 22, who showed up in Kansas to marry his pregnant 14-year-old girlfriend in May. Nebraska Attorney General Jon Bruning rewarded the father-to-be with a rape charge.

Koso's young wife gave birth to a 7-lb, 1-oz girl August 24. Koso faces 50 years in prison on the charge of first-degree sexual assault.[3]

It's the Law: Alabama

In Alabama, it is against the law for a man to seduce "a chaste woman by means of temptation, deception, arts, flattery, or a promise of marriage."[4]

Teen Marriage Stats

The number of married teenagers surged nearly 50 percent during the 1990s, reversing a decades-long decline.

Marriage remains fairly uncommon in this age group—only 4.5% of 15- to 19-year-olds were hitched in 2000—but researchers were nonetheless surprised by the increase reported by the Census Bureau.

David Popenoe of the National Marriage Project at Rutgers University, which studies marriage trends and ways to strengthen marriage, offered several possible reasons.

"There's been a slight trend toward conservatism among teens, less premarital sex, more fear of disease," he said. "It could conceivably have something to do with welfare reform. But it's a surprise."

This generation of teens is the first to live their whole lives with AIDS as a major public health concern. Some counselors suggested wedded teens are taking to heart the "abstinence until marriage" theme projected by some sex education classes.[5]

Common-Law Marriage

A common-law marriage can be created by living together and holding yourselves out as husband and wife for a significant period of time, even if no formal wedding ever took place.

A common-law marriage
occurs when:

- A couple uses the same last name
- You refer to each other as my "husband" or my "wife"
- You file joint tax returns
- You show intent to be married;
- You have continuously lived with each other for seven years (differs by state)
- You and your common law spouse have publicly stated that you are married.[6]

A common-law marriage must be dissolved by divorce the same as a formal marriage.

States with Common-Law Marriages

The following states currently recognize common-law marriages:

Alabama
Colorado
District of Columbia
Iowa
Kansas
Montana
New Hampshire (for inheritance purposes only)[7]
Oklahoma
Pennsylvania
Rhode Island
South Carolina
Texas
Utah

It's the Law: North Carolina

If a man and a woman who aren't married go to a hotel/motel and register themselves as married, then, according to state law, they are legally married.[8]

Marital Support

In marriage today, each spouse is required to provide support to the other and for a child under 18 years of age.

As a result, in many states, you or your spouse can be required to provide necessities to the other, or for your minor children.[10]

Common-Law Marriage

A common-law marriage between a 14-year-old boy and 12-year-old girl is possible after an appellate court ruling this week.

That is the potential fallout from a Colorado Court of Appeals decision that overturned a lower court finding that 15 is too young for a girl to enter into common-law union.

"This is a real shocker," said Stephen Harhai, a Denver attorney and past chairman of the family law section of the Colorado Bar Association. "Under this action, this means your 12-year-old can, with whomever, say, 'I intend to be married to you,' and that's it, (they're) married. That's a little shocking."

The decision by a three-judge panel reversed a Weld County case in which a judge ruled that a 15-year-old girl was too young to consent to a common-law marriage.

It does not alter state law regarding "statutory" or conventional marriage in Colorado, which sets the minimum marriage age at 16 and requires either parental or judicial approval for 16-year-olds and 17-year-olds.[9]

Teen Marriage Stats

• The older a woman is at the time of her first marriage, the longer that marriage is likely to last. That is one of the conclusions of a study based on a 1995 survey by the Centers for Disease Control and Prevention, which looked at 10,847 women ages 15-44.

• Some 43% of first marriages end in either divorce or separation within 15 years—with one in three first marriages dissolving within 10 years, and one in five within five years.[11]

Can A Teen Marriage Last?

It is thought that around 50-60% of all teen marriages will end in divorce. There are many reasons that divorce can be the end result of a teen marriage. First off, most teens will marry for all the wrong reasons. Of course, the teens think that their reasons are well validated.

Pregnancy is a top contender when it comes to why a teen would get married. The teen pregnancy rate is very high in this country. It is estimated that in the United States of America there are 1.3 million babies born out of wedlock each year. Of course this does not include all of the babies born in a teen marriage.

Another reason that a teen would consider marriage is to get out of their parents' home.[12]

Annulment

A marriage can be declared invalid (annulled) if certain conditions exist. Grounds for annulment vary from state to state but generally are:
• Being underage and not having the consent of a parent or guardian
• Lack of legal capacity owing to mental incapacity
• Under the influence of drugs or alcohol
• Physical incapacity to consummate the marriage
• Refusal to consummate the marriage
• Marriage entered into because of force or threat
• Marriage based on a fraudulent act or misrepresentation that goes to the heart of the marriage
• One of the parties is already married
• The marriage is between close relatives
• The marriage is based on concealment of a key matter
• The marriage is based on a material (significant) misunderstanding.[13]

It's the Law: Delaware

In the state of Delaware, getting married on a dare is grounds for an annulment.[14]

Britney's Short Marriage Annulled

Pop star Britney Spears had her surprise marriage annulled, less than 55 hours after tying the knot with a childhood friend.

The singer married Jason Alexander on Saturday morning, during a night out in Las Vegas.

But immediately her lawyers filed for an annulment by the courts.

"Plaintiff Spears lacked understanding of her actions to the extent that she was incapable of agreeing to the marriage," the annulment petition said.

"There is no marriage now," Spears' lawyer David Chesnoff said after the annulment was granted at Clark County Family Court.

"Jason agreed to this completely. They've made a wise decision. I know they care about each other. They are friends," he added.

But Mr. Chesnoff denied Spears was intoxicated when she went through with the ceremony at the Little White Wedding Chapel in Las Vegas.

Ex-husband Alexander has now spoken about the surprise wedding.

"It was just crazy, man," he told Access Hollywood.

"We were just looking at each other and said, 'Let's do something wild, crazy. Let's go get married, just for the hell of it'."

He added that they soon realized that they had to fix the "mistake" they had made.

An annulment dissolves a marriage as if it never took place, while a divorce would have recognized that it did occur.

Court information officer Michael Sommermeyer read out the reasons why the annulment was sought.

"Before entering into the marriage, the plaintiff and defendant did not know each other's likes and dislikes, each other's desires to have or not have children, and each other's desires as to state of residency.

"Upon learning of each other's desires, they are so incompatible that there was a want of understanding of each other's actions in entering into this marriage."[15]

Community Property

States with community property laws define community property as:
- All assets and wages earned during your marriage
- All assets and wages obtained during your marriage
- Equal control and ownership of community property between spouses[16]

Separate Property

The following items are considered separate property and are not subject to community property laws:
- Anything you owned prior to marriage
- Anything you inherited during the marriage
- Any gift you received during the marriage
- Anything either spouse earned after the date of their separation
- A legal settlement to one spouse
- A legal judgment to one spouse

These items should also have been kept separate from the community property.[17]

Divorce: Separation Agreement

The parties may (on their own) enter into a separation agreement to settle the issues related to their divorce. A judge will review such an agreement to make certain it is fair to the parties and to any minor children.

The court is required to make decisions based on the "best interests of the children." The court will:
- Allocate parental responsibilities
- Allocate one parent all or part of the decision-making responsibility of the children for:
- All areas, or
- For only special areas, such as education and/or medical
- Allocate parenting time
- Determine child support.[18]

Divorce Petition

To dissolve your marriage, you have to file a divorce petition. It is best to consult with an attorney knowledgeable in marital law.

In the divorce proceeding, if the parties cannot agree, a judge or mediator will decide:
- Financial support for either spouse
- Custody of children
- Support for children
- Division of property

In most instances, community property is divided equally between spouses, including their debts. [19]

Grounds for Fault Divorce

Grounds for divorce differ from state to state. Some frequent grounds for divorce are:

- Incurable insanity
- Irreconcilable differences
- Separation (for a set period of time)
- Irreconcilable breakdown of a marriage
- Complete incompatibility of temperament
- Incapacity
- Adultery
- Physical violence
- Mental cruelty
- Imprisonment (for a period of time)
- Addiction
- Habitual drunkenness
- Habitual use of drugs
- Bigamy
- Conviction of a heinous crime
- Intolerable cruelty
- Impotency
- Infection of spouse with a STD
- Non-support
- Sodomy or buggery outside of marriage
- Imprisonment for life
- Seven year absence or unheard from
- Attempt on life of spouse by poisoning or other means of showing malice
- Deviant sexual conduct voluntarily performed by defendant without consent of the plaintiff

Grounds for Husband Only

- Wife's pregnancy at the time of marriage without the knowledge or agency of the husband

Grounds For Wife Only

- Non-support for two years

It's the Law: Kansas

In Wichita, Kansas, a man's mistreatment of his mother-in-law may not be used as grounds for divorce.[20]

No Fault Divorce

No fault divorce means in seeking a divorce you merely have to allege that the marriage is "irretrievably broken," there are "irreconcilable differences," "incompatibility," or an "irremediable breakdown of the marriage" depending on your state.

Neither spouse blames the other for the breakdown of the marriage. Both spouses agree that irreconcilable differences have arisen, and that neither time nor counseling will save the marriage. The marriage simply will not work.

Therefore, fault is not an issue.

It's the Law: Minnesota

No man is allowed to make love to his wife with the smell of garlic, onions, or sardines on his breath in Alexandria, Minnesota. If his wife so requests, law mandates that he must brush his teeth.[21]

Divorce: Mediation

Frequently a couple cannot work out the terms related to their divorce. If so, the couple can go into mediation with a trained mediator to try to resolve the issues, or the court may order them to do so.

If after mediation the couple cannot agree, they can go to court and a judge will decide for them.

Rights Upon Divorce

Upon your divorce, the court granting the divorce may order:
- **Spousal Support:** Either party may be required to pay support to the other for a period determined by the court.
- **Child Support:** Either or both parties may be required to pay for the support of their children.
- **Division of Marital Property:** There may be an equitable division of all marital property.
- **Equitable Division**: It is not necessarily an equal division—it depends on:
  - The length of the marriage
  - Contributions of the parties to the marriage
  - The earning capabilities of the parties
  - Other factors[22]

Loss Of Parental Rights

You can lose your right as a parent for:
- Failure to assume financial responsibility
- Failure to assume moral responsibility
- Abandonment
- Repeated abuse
- A continuing need for protection for the child
- Endangering the parental relationship and therefore:
  - The child's safety
  - The child's health
  - The child's development
- Being unable or unwilling to eliminate harm facing the child
- Being unable or unwilling to provide a safe and stable home
- Severe or chronic abuse or neglect
- Long-term mental illness or deficiency of the parents
- Long-term alcohol or drug-induced incapacity
- The involuntary termination of rights of a parent to another child
- Failure to maintain contact with a child
- Felony conviction for a crime of violence against a child or another family member
- Conviction of a felony when the term is so long it will have a negative impact on a child and the only available source of care is foster care
- Doing more harm than good.

Doing More Harm Than Good

February 27, 2007—British authorities may take an 8-year-old boy weighing 99kg (3 times the normal weight for his age) away from his mother unless his mother improves his diet.

Basic Child Custody Facts

- The court makes the final decision to safeguard the child against acute or chronic feelings of guilt.
- In most states, the court will consider the child's wishes differently based on the child's age.
- In a situation involving more than one child, experts feel that it is usually best to keep all siblings together with respect to the custody arrangements.
- Divorce splits the bond of husband and wife, and custody splits the bond of parenting.[23]

Divorce: Parenting Time

Based on the best interest of the children, all relevant factors for the children's welfare are considered to determine parenting time, such as:

- Will of the children
- Relationship between the child and parents
- Ability of the parent to encourage the sharing of love, affection, and contact between the child and each parent.

The sex of a parent is not to be taken into account by the court in making its parenting time decisions. For example, a mother should not be deemed more suited to raise children than the father based on being a female.

In some cases, the court will request a qualified professional to make evaluations of the parents, children, and circumstances to make a recommendation to the court.

Child Custody: Types

The different types of child custody are:

- **Physical Custody**: denotes where the child lives
- **Legal Custody**: gives a person the authority to make important decisions for a child, for their medical treatment, education, and religion
- **Sole Physical Custody**: when a child lives with only one parent
- **Joint Physical Custody**: when a child lives part-time with each parent
- **Sole Legal Custody**: only one parent makes all of the important decisions about the child.
- **Joint Legal Custody**: when both parents share in the decision-making authority

Domestic Violence/Abuse

Domestic abuse is an assault that occurs in certain relationships. It is domestic abuse when the assault:

- Is between a divorced or separated couple who no longer live together
- Is between family members or persons who live in the same household at the time of the assault
- Is between persons who have a child together, regardless of whether they ever lived together or were married
- Is between people who lived together in the prior year but are not living together at the time the assault occurs.

It occurs if the family member, partner, or ex-partner attempts to physically or psychologically dominate or harm the other.[24]

Relief from Domestic Abuse

Usually you can file a petition in court for relief from domestic abuse.

If a petition is granted, the judge can issue a temporary order to protect the victim from further abuse until the hearing can be held.

Domestic Violence

Domestic Violence includes:
Domestic abuse
Economic deprivation
Emotional abuse
Family violence
Husband battery
Incest
Intimidation
Physical violence
Relationship violence
Sexual abuse
Spiritual violation
Spousal abuse
Spouse beating
Stalking
Threat of violence
Wife battery

A judge is usually always on call, even on weekends and at night to handle these petitions. In most cases, a hearing is held within ten (10) days of the filing of the petition.

At the hearing the judge has many available remedies. The judge could order:

- The abuse to stop
- The abuser out of the family home
- The abuser to stay away from the victim
- Temporary custody of children to the victim or another
- Monetary support to the victim.
- Violation of orders in contempt of court are subject to jail.

In many jurisdictions, a violation of a no-contact order can result in a jail time of seven (7) days or more.

Duty of Law Enforcement

If a legal officer has reason to think domestic abuse has occurred, the officer is required to use all reasonable means to stop further domestic abuse. This means the officer must remain at the scene, if required. The police must:

- Assist victims who need medical attention
- Provide victims with numbers of shelters or help lines
- Provide a list of rights to victims

Abuser Uncertainty

If a police officer cannot decide who the abuser or the aggressor is, the police can arrest both parties.

- No arrest warrant is necessary for an abuser if there is probable cause to believe a domestic assault has taken place.
- Police generally are required to make an arrest if bodily injury has occurred, if the aggressor has attempted to inflict serious injury, or if the aggressor has used a dangerous weapon.
- You will not be arrested if you inflict injury in self-defense.

Unmarried Parents

If the parents of a child are unmarried at the time of the child's birth, both the mother and father must consent to have the father's name added to the child's birth certificate.

The court can decide issues of parental rights and obligations when the biological parents are not married. Both parents have a legal obligation to support their child. Both are entitled to contact and visit their child. The court can establish requirements for child support, visitation rights, etc.[27]

Domestic Abuse Stats

Approximately 1.3 million women and 835,000 men are physically assaulted by an intimate partner annually in the United States.[25]

Intimate partner violence made up 20% of all non-fatal violent crime experienced by women in 2001.

In 2000, 1,247 women and 440 men were killed by an intimate partner. In recent years, an intimate partner killed approximately 33% of female murder victims and 4% of male murder victims.[26]

Establishing Paternity

You can bring a legal action in court to try to establish paternity or parental rights. You could do this to:
- Establish your parental rights
- Prove a person has fathered your child

Home and Visitation

In a paternity suit, the judge can also select the proper home for the child and a visitation schedule.

Mediation

These types of actions are, as a rule, first subject to mediation. If that fails, the matter will be heard in court.[28]

Proving Paternity

A person can file a legal complaint to establish parental rights. After paternity tests, the court can then rule on child support, visitation, and related rights.[29]

Chapter Nineteen
INTERNET, COMPUTER USE, AND TELEMARKETERS

• • • • • • • •

Internet and Computer Use

When you are on the Internet you should always assume that anyone in the world has access to what you are communicating. Do not include anything that you would not want to read on the front page of your local newspaper. Do not be lulled into a false sense of security that what you transmit is private and can be eliminated easily by hitting the delete button on your computer—that is seldom the case.

It is important for you to exercise great caution when you access the Internet on any computer. Always set your personal profiles to private and limit the number of people who can access them. Limit the number and type of photos you post, and choose them carefully, as anyone can use them at anytime in the future. Do not let your friends jeopardize your personal information—check routinely how they use your information online.

Social Networking Sites: Safety Tips

The advent of social networking sites such as Facebook and MySpace have raised a whole new series of legal and personal risks for you.

The FTC suggests these tips for socializing safely online:

- Think about how different sites work before deciding to join a site. Some sites will allow only a defined community of users to access posted content; others allow anyone and everyone to view postings.
- Think about keeping some control over the information you post. Consider restricting access to your page to a select group of people, for example, your friends from school, your club, your team, your community groups, or your family.
- Keep your personal information to yourself. Don't post your full name, Social Security Number, address, phone number, or bank and credit card account numbers—and do not post other people's information, either. Be cautious about posting information that could be used to identify you or locate you offline. This could include the name of your school, sports team, clubs, and where you work or hang out.
- Make sure your screen name does not contain too much information about you. Do not use your name, your age, or your hometown. Even if you think your screen name makes you anonymous, it does not take a genius to combine clues to figure out who you are and where you can be found.
- Post only information that you are comfortable with others seeing—and knowing—about you. Many people can see your page, including your parents, your teachers, the police, the college you might want to apply to next year, or the employer for the job you might want to apply for in five years.

Meeting Someone in Person

If you are interested in meeting someone you met online in person, bring a friend or parent and meet in a very open and public place during the day. Never go alone.[1]

Busted

It should be obvious, but do not break into your school's computer system to alter grades.

A Florida high school senior and class president has been arrested for allegedly breaking into his school's computer system and altering student's grades. Ryan C. Shrouder allegedly used a school board employee's password to gain access to the system. He will be suspended and recommended for expulsion. Two other students have been suspended in connection with the case.[5]

- Remember that once you post information online, you cannot take it back. Even if you delete the information from a site, older versions exist on other people's computers. Do not assume anything can be completely deleted.
- Consider not posting your photo. It can be altered and broadcast in ways you may not be happy about. If you do post one, ask yourself whether it is one your mom would display in the living room.
- Flirting with strangers online could have serious consequences. Because some people lie about who they really are, you never really know who you are dealing with.
- Be suspicious if a new online friend wants to meet you in person. Before you decide to meet someone, do your research. Ask whether any of your friends know the person, and see what background you can dig up through online search engines. If you decide to meet them, be smart about it. Meet in a public place, during the day, with friends you trust. Tell an adult or a responsible sibling where you are going and when you expect to be back.
- Trust your gut if you have suspicions. If you feel threatened by someone or uncomfortable because of something online, tell an adult you trust and report it to the police and the social networking site. You could end up preventing someone else from becoming a victim.[2]

Busted

A study last year found that half the nation's teens—12 million youths—have created content on the Internet. That includes blogs, personal web pages, photo sites, or similar online handiwork.

Officials at MySpace, one of the most popular social networking sites, say they frequently assist police in investigations. The site also offers safety advice for users and their parents.

Two months ago, after a 17-year-old was charged with allegedly having an assault-style rifle outside an East Mecklenburgh High football game, a Charlotte crime blogger posted photographs of that teen and more than a dozen others posing either with guns or flashing gang signs. The photographs, according to the blog, were taken from MySpace, and depicted Charlotte-area teens.

Police Department Captain, Eddie Levins, said it is not illegal to pose with a gun, unless you are a convicted felon. Even then, he said, it would be difficult to prove that the gun is real.

"There are air soft guns that look just like real guns," he said. Getting a conviction would require more proof than a MySpace picture, he said.

But police across the country are using the Internet as part of criminal investigations:
- In Pennsylvania, police used photographs posted on Webshots.com to place teenage crash victims at a party where beer and rum were served, according to court documents.
- In Colorado, a 16-year-old was charged with illegal gun possession after authorities said he posted photos on MySpace showing himself holding guns.
- Police at Penn State used Facebook to identify unruly football fans who rushed the field after a win against Ohio State.

Dr. Phyllis B. Gerstenfeld, chair of the criminal justice department at California State University, said that sites are not an ideal investigative tool because people can lie online. However, many workers have lost jobs and students have gotten into trouble as a result of what they have posted, she said.[3]

Busted

Of course, how you use your computer and online access must be lawful.

Two teenagers in New York State have been taken into police custody on charges of illegal computer access and attempted extortion after they allegedly threatened to shake down the website MySpace.com unless its operators paid them $150,000, prosecutors said.

Shaun Harrison, 18, and Saverio Mondelli, 19, of Suffolk County, allegedly hacked into the popular social networking site and stole personal information from MySpace users.

After MySpace banned them from the site, the pair threatened to distribute a foolproof method for stealing information unless MySpace paid them $150,000, said Sandi Gibbons, a spokeswoman for the Los Angeles County district attorney's office. MySpace is based in Santa Monica, California.

Mondelli and Harrison were arrested…when they traveled to Los Angeles, allegedly to collect the payoff. Instead, they were taken into custody by undercover officers from the multi-agency Electronic Crimes Task Force, who posed as MySpace employees. Each was charged with two felony counts of illegal computer access and one count of sending a threatening letter for extortion and attempted extortion. They face more than four years in prison if convicted of all charges, prosecutors said.[4]

Posting is Forever

It is important for you to realize that anything you post online, while editable, can be saved while it is live. Any user can save, keep, or distribute photos or text from a web page. This means that sexually suggestive photos, pictures depicting drug use, gang signs, threats against others, or language indicating criminal behavior are all potentially permanent collector's items for your classmates, friends, enemies, parents, total strangers, and law enforcement officials.[6]

Do not post illegal, reckless, or irresponsible acts of your own or others on the Internet.

Busted

Why would someone commit a crime then post it on YouTube?

The local authorities arrested a Pike County, KY, teen after YouTube published numerous videos with the 18-year-old student vandalizing several stores. It seems like this was not the only accusation because the movies showed him breaking church windows and menacing drive-through restaurant workers.

"Charles Jeremy Brown, a high school senior, was charged with 27 counts of menacing, eight counts of criminal mischief, and one count of criminal littering after investigators watched 46 videos starring Brown and three or four others on the YouTube website, said Pike County Chief Deputy sheriff Melvin Sayers. Brown was being held in the Pike County Detention Center last night," the same publication added.[8]

Internet Safety

It is important to remain vigilant to many of the dangers that exist on the Internet. You should be on the lookout for:

- **Identity Theft**: Do not disclose your bank account number or credit card number unless you have initiated the contact and it is over a secure site (secure URLs start with https://). Do not disclose other personal or financial information on the Internet.
- **Spamming:** Do not open or reply to spam e-mail that is sent from someone unknown to you. If you reply, you verify your e-mail address, which can expose you to further risks and subsequent e-mail lists and scams.
- **Predators:** Be especially careful of chat rooms and bulletin boards when you communicate with people who are unknown to you. Pedophiles and other sexual predators frequently misrepresent who they are. Do not agree to meet face-to-face with them or to provide sexually explicit pictures of yourself.
- **Downloads:** Do not download anything to your computer unless you are positive it is from a trustworthy source. When in doubt, do not download. Downloads can be used to:
  1. Plant viruses
  2. Display unwanted advertisements
  3. Track what you are doing online
  4. Expose your computer to further hacking threats
- **Privacy:** If you are not careful online, inappropriate people may get access to your private/personal information, which could then be used improperly. Do not write anything in reply to an e-mail that you would not want repeated to your parents or the public.
- **Viruses, Worms, and Trojan Horses:** A Virus is a piece of computer code that attaches itself to a program or file so it can spread from computer to computer. A Worm is a virus that can spread without any other action being done by you. A Trojan Horse is a malware program that appears useful but actually facilitates unauthorized access to your computer system.
- **Improper Material:** It is easy to innocently wander into a highly offensive site dedicated to extremist groups, sexist, or racist content. If you do so, you should obviously leave the site at once.[7]

Busted

Do not use your computer skills to infest the computers of others with viruses.

Jeffrey Lee Parson, the Minnesota teenager charged with unleashing the W32. Blaster-B Internet worm, is free on bail after a hearing…in federal court in St. Paul, MN.

Parson, an 18-year-old from Hopkins, MN, was arrested…in connection with the release of a variant of the Blaster worm. The FBI and Secret Service conducted a joint investigation to catch the virus writer, according to FBI spokesperson Bill Murray.

Parson was released on a $25,000 personal recognizance bond and directed to appear before a magistrate judge in Seattle…according to Pat Sabin, deputy clerk at the St. Paul court. Parson was not required to put up any money to be released but will need to keep court officers informed of his whereabouts, Sabin says.

In addition, Parson must wear an electronic monitoring device and be confined to his home except to attend school, receive medical treatment, and make court appearances, she says. The court also has barred Parson from accessing the Internet and has forbidden him to use computer or "connected devices" at his home or any other location, Sabin says.[9]

Internet Shopping: Exercise Caution

Internet shopping is very convenient and easy, but you must constantly exercise caution and follow certain safeguards when buying items online:

- Always use a browser that is secure. A secure browser may come with your computer; if not, you can download one for free. The browser scrambles the purchasing information.
- Do not send any of your personal information over the Internet unless you see the secure lock icon.
- Do not share your password with anyone. Make sure it is at least eight (8) characters long and, if possible, has a combination of numbers, letters (multiple cases), and symbols.
- Shop only on sites that you are familiar with. View their refund and return policies before you order anything.

Online Credit Card Purchase

If you use a credit card for your online purchases:

- You are protected by the Fair Credit Billing Act.
- You can dispute charges if the item you purchased does not arrive or is not as represented.
- You can stop payment while your credit card company investigates your claim.
- If your credit card is misused, your liability is limited to $50.00.
- Some credit card companies even offer a guarantee so that you are not responsible for the unauthorized use of your card.[10]

Busted

A mid-Missouri teen faces 25 years in prison for Internet fraud.

Attorney General Jay Nixon and the Miller County prosecutor said 18-year-old Joseph Merkle of Eldon began advertising computers and computer equipment for sale on the Internet in January 2002.

Merkle allegedly told customers to wire him money but never sent them their purchases.

Merkle faces five charges of consumer fraud and is currently being held in the Miller County Jail on more than $4,000 bond.[11]

Lost Credit Card

If you lose, misplace, or have your credit card stolen, notify your credit card company immediately. Keep a record of the credit car company's phone number for this purpose.

Keep written records of your purchases.

The Mail or Telephone Order Rule requires that a merchant who advertises has a reasonable basis for stating or implying that he can ship within a certain time. If the seller makes no shipment statement, he must have a reasonable basis for believing that he can ship within 30 days. That is why direct marketers sometimes call this the "30 Day Rule."

If the seller, after taking your order learns he cannot ship within the time he stated, or within 30 days, he must seek your consent to the delayed shipment. If he cannot obtain your consent, for any reason, he must, without being asked, promptly refund the money you paid.

Busted

It seems obvious, but do not threaten illegal conduct on MySpace or elsewhere.

A high school senior was arrested after he threatened to blow up his private school on the popular MySpace.com website, authorities said.

Deputies say they searched Brian Hall, 18, at Sonrise Christian School on Friday and found a set of brass knuckles and a knife.

When deputies searched Hall's vehicle, they found two more knives and a pipe with marijuana residue inside...

Hall was booked in county jail. He was charged with having a weapon on school property, and drug possession...

The teen had a clock-like icon on MySpace that was, according to the website, counting down the hours until he supposedly was going to destroy Sonrise Christian School, the Sheriff's Office said.[12]

Busted

Guaranteed 2,000% return should have been a red flag.

American authorities have settled a lawsuit with a California teenager who allegedly swindled investors out of more than $900,000 by operating a fraudulent investment service website.

The Securities and Exchange Commission claimed in a civil lawsuit that 17-year-old Cole Bartiromo, who still lives with his parents, defrauded about 1,000 investors through his "Invest Better 2001" site, which has now been removed from the web.

As part of the settlement, the teenager will be forced to pay back the money the SEC says he made from the website and stashed in an account in a Costa Rican casino.

He has never openly confirmed or denied the SEC's allegations.

Mr. Bartiromo allegedly sold what he described as "guaranteed" and "risk-free" products in which he invested clients' funds to bet on sporting events.

The SEC said Mr. Bartiromo had guaranteed returns of up to 2,000% for investors.

However, the New York Times reported that although some early investors did receive returns, the scheme began to fail in December last year and disgruntled clients began to complain on the site's message boards that their money had gone missing.[13]

Identity Theft

The theft of people's identity, primarily from e-mails and the Internet, is a major area of current crime. You have to be continually alert so criminals cannot discover your personal information.

To help protect your identity:
- Do not lose or misplace your purse and/or wallet.
- Shred important documents before you put them in the garbage.
- Make sure no one can access your credit cards or credit card numbers.
- Do not respond to suspicious or phony e-mail.
- Be alert to phony websites, especially those that request you to provide your Social Security Number, bank account information, or driver's license number at the outset, especially if you did not initiate the contact.
- Do not carry your Social Security Number with you—memorize it.
- Shred credit card offers received in the mail.
- Stop pre-approved credit card offers.
- Do not give out personal information to solicitors on the phone, mail, or e-mail.
- Use firewalls and virus-scanning software on your computer.

- Use computer passwords of at least eight characters long with a combination of numbers, symbols, and letters.
- Only download software from trusted sites.
- Do not use spyware software.
- Do not open spam e-mail.
- Do not open pop-up windows.
- Check your bills and bank statements for accuracy as soon as you receive them. Report any unknown or incorrect item.
- Look carefully for unusual, unknown, or unauthorized charges, purchases, or withdrawals.
- Check with your bank if you do not receive your bank statements timely, as it could have been removed from your mail.
- Ask questions if you are asked for personal information that seems inappropriate for the transaction. If you do not get proper replies, do business elsewhere.
- Request a free credit report from one of three credit companies each year. These are Experian.com, (800-397-3742), Equifax.com (800-685-1111), and Transunion.com (800-888-4213).
- Do not leave your mail in unsecured mailboxes
- Place your outgoing mail only in United States Postal Service mail boxes or post offices.
- Never leave receipts at gas pumps, stores, ATMs, etc.
- Use only secure internet sites when making purchases.
- Before you purchase anything from a website, make certain the lock icon appears at the bottom of a web page and the letters "HTTPS" are at the beginning of the URL. The "s" is for secure.[14]

Identity Theft Stats

The Federal Trade Commission reports that young people make up 31% of reported cases of identity theft each year. This is because they have unblemished credit records (indeed, they have no credit record at all!) Once their identity is stolen, it can go undetected for months, if not years, and teenagers and children are likely to be ignorant to any signs that their identity has been compromised.[15]

The 18-year-old New Zealander's screen name is "AKILL," and he is the alleged head "of an international cyber crime network accused of infiltrating 1.3 million computers" and stealing $20+ million from victims' bank accounts…

"Working with the FBI and police in the Netherlands, New Zealand police raided his house in Hamilton and took him and several computers in custody." His arrest was part of an international crackdown on criminal hackers who hack or social-engineer their way into large numbers of computers, install malicious software, and take control of the machines, turning them into zombies. The zombie computers become part of large networks (or botnets) of computers that can launch denial-of-service attacks on large commercial websites, extort, manipulate stocks, etc. "Eight people have been indicted, pleaded guilty, or have been convicted since the investigation started in June."[16]

Identity Theft

Identity theft victims have had some of the following happen to them as a direct result of their identity being stolen:

- They have been denied employment owing to failed background checks.
- They have been turned down for insurance, or charged higher premiums.
- They have had their credit cards canceled, or their rates jacked up to astronomical rates.
- They have been denied housing because of negative items on their credit reports.
- They have been turned down for mortgages, after saving for years for the down payment.
- Some people have even been arrested because of the thief's action!

Some people have to spend thousands of dollars and countless months working to restore their credit and their lives. It is not something to be taken lightly. You could lose your job, your credit, or even your home if you are the victim of identity theft!

You might even be arrested, and the charges can sometimes be difficult to defend against if you have no proof that it was not you who committed the crime.

Norfolk Southern says a Chesapeake teenager found a clever new use for his home computer: he allegedly downloaded the railroad's logo from the Internet, used WordPerfect to create fake purchase orders, faxed them to vendors, and got $7,000 in computer equipment billed to Norfolk Southern.

He is now in a Florida jail, awaiting extradition to Virginia.

Norfolk Southern police said they have charged the young man—Kenneth Michael Martin, 19, of Princess Anne Crescent in Chesapeake—with three felonies: computer fraud, obtaining property under false pretenses, and fraud or forgery of a document.

Norfolk Southern caught up with Martin when one vendor checked the order and found it was fake, Simpkins said. He said he got the young man's name when Martin signed for a Federal Express package.[17]

Busted

Social Internet sites are routinely prowled by law enforcement officials for illegal activities.

Florida law enforcement agencies, backed by hundreds of thousands of dollars in state grants, now are patrolling the Internet in the same way officers have traditionally pounded the streets of their beats.

Investigators have been seeking out online sexual predators for years. But experts say the number of officers searching for cyberspace crimes is rapidly rising as they turn social networking websites, such as Facebook.com and MySpace.com into their personal beats.

Last week, in what is believed to be the first drug bust in the area that used website monitoring, Punta Gorda police arrested a teenager who boasted on a MySpace webpage of smoking marijuana.

The Sarasota County Sheriff's Office conducted its first successful online sex predator sting this year, and three Sarasota police detectives work computer investigations full time.

"We have to go where the criminals are," said Mike Phillips, special agent supervisor with the Florida Department of Law Enforcement Computer Crime Center.

Law enforcement officers have found criminals who used to rob banks committing identify theft online, Phillips said. Because children have been taught not to talk to strangers, child molesters who stalked bus stops have turned to popular teen sites such as MySpace.com.

"I think the increase in the use of the Internet and criminals using the Internet have driven our administration to realize we needed more manpower," Phillips said.

It has been argued that some of the nation's tragedies, such as the Columbine High School massacre and the terrorist attack of September 11, 2001, could have been avoided if law enforcement had made use of available technology, said Hollinger, an expert on computer crimes.

Children do not expect police to be scavenging their webpages, but their expectation of privacy on the Internet would not be recognized in court, said Paul Sullivan, a local defense attorney.

People cannot keep police from snooping around Internet sites that any other member of the public can look at, he added.

"It's part of the world we live in, where you think of the Internet as a private sanctuary. But in reality it's terribly public," Sullivan said. "People are just going to have to change their way of thinking about what they do on the Internet."

An undercover detective used the MySpace website to find, contact, and set up a deal with the teen to buy 2 ounces of marijuana, according to an arrest report. The teen was arrested Tuesday when he showed up with the drugs.[18]

Telemarketers

Fraudulent telemarketers often pose as representatives of well-known sweepstakes. Consumers are being told through calls and letters (supposedly from the major sweepstakes) that they have won valuable prizes. They are then asked to provide money to take care of processing fees, prepayment of taxes, or handling charges. They are told to send the funds by overnight delivery service or Western Union.

Scam Tip-Offs

Being asked to pay money up-front for a prize is a sure tip-off to a scam.

Insisting on overnight delivery of money to the sweepstakes is another clue to a fraudulent operation. A quick response lessens the time the consumer can consider the offer or check on the source. Using a courier service to send the money avoids the possibility of mail fraud charges.

Asking for your credit card number to verify eligibility. Consumers are advised never to give financial information over the phone to an unfamiliar caller. The number may be used to make unauthorized purchases which will later appear on credit card bills.

If you are told that you have won a sweepstakes prize, call the appropriate number below to make sure the unlikely news is true.
- Publishers Clearing House: 1-800-337-4724
- American Family Publishers: 1-800-237-2400
- Reader's Digest Sweepstakes: 1-800-234-9000[19]

Busted

A not-so-wise cottage industry.

Police say a 19-year-old, working out of a tiny cottage overlooking Lake Quinsigamond, used the Internet to bilk customers all over the country and Canada out of $30,000 to $40,000.

The accused, Michael R. Deppe, says all the transactions were legitimate, part of a brisk business he has conducted online since he was 13 years old. Deppe was indicted on 15 counts of larceny, including failing to deliver promised goods such as a Rolex watch, a plasma television, a digital video recorder, sports memorabilia, and six tickets to a Celine Dion concert with airfare and lodging at Caesar's Palace in Las Vegas. Deppe was also charged with one count of identity fraud.[20]

Busted

Internet scams and crimes are taking many different forms.

The Craigslist ad was as hot as the car it was trying to sell.

A turbocharged "stunning Carmona red" 2007 Porsche 911 whose owner was unloading it for $60,000, half the usual sticker price.

But when would-be buyers showed up to see the sports coupe, a girl-led group of teens robbed them of their cash.

The mastermind behind the internet scam, which used plagiarized postings and photos from Craigslist ads, was a 17-year-old resident of Maspeth, Queens, Agniesika Banach, Nassau County police said.

Banach, a student at the High School for Environmental Studies in Manhattan, enlisted the help of six male friends, ages 16 to 19, who acted as the muscle in two strong-arm robberies, the cops said.

"You have a 17-year-old student scheming in her home, knowing that people will jump at a bargain that is too good to be true, and using the Internet to lure her victims, said Nassau Police Detective Lt. Karl Schoepp.

In one instance, a Pennsylvania couple who thought they had found a steal on Craigslist drove to Freeport, Long Island, on November 26 to meet the owner of the half-price Porsche.

The teen thugs beat and robbed the husband and wife of the $4,000 they had brought as a down payment.

Schoepp said Banach had "directed the operation" by posting the ads, recruiting her cohorts, and corresponding with the victims via e-mail and with the type of prepaid cell phone that "you can buy at 7-Eleven."

Police arrested Banach on December 17 after getting her e-mail address by subpoenaing Craigslist and her Internet provider.

Through interviews and the seizing of her computer, cops were able to track down and arrest her six alleged accomplices.[22]

Internet Scams

There are also an ever-increasing number of Internet scams that you have to be alert to. Some of the most used ones are:

- False representation of charities: Make-A-Wish, etc.
- Internet dating solicitations
- Lottery scams
- Missed jury duty service, need your personal information
- PayPal: missed payment
- Nigerian government seeking your help[21]

Chapter Twenty
CREDIT RATING AND BANKRUPTCY

● ● ● ● ● ● ● ●

Your Credit Rating

It is important when you turn 18, or earlier, to establish a good credit rating as soon as you can. You should:
- Open and maintain a savings account
- Get a job
- Buy low cost items on credit
- Use a credit card in low amounts and pay your bill on time

Your credit rating establishes your ability to pay debt.

To establish credit, you need a record of making your credit payments on time, a stable source of income, and/or other sources of funds.[1]

Start establishing credit as early as possible by obtaining a credit card and paying your invoices timely and monthly.

If You Bounce a Check

If you bounce a check by issuing a check for more money than you have in your checking account:

- The bank could return the check to the person who cashed/or attempted to cash it.
- If you know you did not have adequate funds in your checking account when you wrote the check, you could be charged with a fine.
- The person to whom you wrote the check could charge you up to three (3) times the amount of the check in penalties.
- The bank may go ahead and pay the check, charge you a penalty, and require you to make a deposit to cover the check plus the penalty.[2]

Do not write checks if you do not have enough funds in your account to cover the amount of the check. You can obtain a checking account with overdraft privileges to cover checks written for more than you can cover in your account. The interest charges for these overdraft accounts are usually quite high. It is best to discipline yourself to only write checks for the funds you have available to avoid poor financial practices.

Know Your Balance

You are responsible for knowing the balance in your account at all times before you issue a check, or for any account that you issue funds from for that matter.

Equal Credit Opportunity

The Equal Credit Opportunity Act (ECOA) ensures that all consumers are given an equal chance to obtain credit.

Under the ECOA if you apply for credit, a creditor may not:

- Discourage you from applying because of your sex, marital status, age, race, national origin, or because you receive public assistance income.
- Ask you to reveal your sex, race, national origin, or religion.
- Ask if you are widowed or divorced. When permitted to ask marital status, a creditor may only use the terms: married, unmarried, or separated.
- Ask about your marital status if you are applying for a separate, unsecured account. A creditor may ask you to provide this information if you live in community property states: Arizona, California, Idaho, Louisiana, Nevada, New Mexico, Texas, and Washington. A creditor in any state may ask for this information if you apply for a joint account or one secured by property.
- Request information about your spouse, except when your spouse is applying with you, your spouse will be allowed to use the account, you are relying on your spouse's income or on alimony or child support income from a former spouse, or if you reside in a community property state.
- Inquire about your plans for having or raising children.
- Ask if you receive alimony, child support, or separate maintenance payments, unless you will not rely on these payments to get credit. A creditor may ask if you have to pay alimony, child support, or separate maintenance payments.

When deciding to give you credit, a creditor may not:

- Consider your sex, marital status, race, national origin, or religion.
- Consider whether you have a telephone listing in your name. A creditor may consider whether you have a phone.
- Consider the race of people in the neighborhood where you want to buy, refinance, or improve a house with borrowed money.
- Consider your age, unless you are too young to sign contracts— generally younger than 18 years of age.[3]

Debt Collection Pointers

Your Employer: Debt collectors are permitted to contact your employer by letter requesting verification of your employment and location only. A debt collector cannot ask your employer for your pay or other personal information.

Deception: A debt collector cannot make any false representation or use deceptive means to collect or attempt to collect any debt or to obtain information concerning you.

Surcharges: A debt collector cannot add surcharges to your debt for interest, charge late fees, service charges, bad check handling fees, or expenses unless they are expressly authorized by your agreement, or if your contract is silent on such indicated charges if expressly permitted by your states' law. Conversely, if the state law expressly prohibits collection of certain additional items, if your agreement is silent on the subject, the item cannot be collected.

Challenge Incorrect Information

Do not fail to challenge or correct inaccurate information on your credit report.

Credit Repair Scams

If you decide to respond to a credit repair offer, look for these telltale signs of a scam:

- Companies that want you to pay for credit repair services before they provide any services.
- Companies that do not tell you your legal rights and what you can do for yourself for free.
- Companies that recommend that you not contact a credit reporting company directly.
- Companies that suggest that you try to invent a "new" credit identity—and then, a new credit report—by applying for an Employer Identification Number to use instead of your Social Security Number.
- Companies that advise you to dispute all information in your credit report or take any action that seems illegal, like creating a new credit identity. If you follow illegal advice and commit fraud you may be subject to prosecution.

False Information

You could be charged and prosecuted for mail or wire fraud if you use the mail or telephone to apply for credit and provide false information. It is a federal crime to lie on a loan or credit application, to misrepresent your Social Security Number, or to obtain an Employer Identification Number from the Internal Revenue Service under false pretenses.

Under the Credit Repair Organizations Act, credit repair companies cannot require you to pay until they have completed the services they have promised.[6]

Your Credit Report

Check your credit report at least once a year (please see page 140).

Personal Bankruptcy

If you file for personal bankruptcy, you are usually required to turn over to the bankruptcy court all of your assets. These assets, with certain exceptions, will be your real and personal property. These assets will be used by the bankruptcy court to help pay your creditors the money you owe them.

Discharged

After the proceedings in bankruptcy are completed, you will obtain a discharge. Discharge means in most instances that your debts are extinguished.[7]

Your Credit Standing

A bankruptcy proceeding will damage your credit standing and will make it more difficult to secure credit in the future.

Bankruptcy actions are noted in your credit record for at least ten (10) years.

Bankruptcy: Non-Cancellable Debts

Even after a formal bankruptcy proceeding, some debts cannot be cancelled. These are:

- Debts for taxes
- Debts not reported by you to the bankruptcy court
- Educational loans
- Debts you obtained via fraud
- Debts for intentional or malicious injury, or damages to people or property.[8]

Chapter Twenty-One
YOUR ESTATE

● ● ● ● ● ● ● ●

Planning Your Estate

Although no one likes to consider estate planning (how you plan to distribute and handle your assets after your death), part of turning 18 should prompt such planning. If nothing else, it makes things easier for your family and friends in the event of your death.

Estate planning is necessary and useful because:
- If you have children, it will provide who will be their guardian.
- You can provide for your medical care via advance directives if you become incapacitated.
- By planning in advance you can reduce:
  - Your estate taxes
  - Your gift taxes
  - Your income taxes
- It provides for the orderly transfer of your:
  - Property
  - Business
  - Pets[1]

Retirement Plans

Retirement plans from employment arrangements are not part of your will because these plans require you to specify your beneficiaries in advance.

Examples of retirement plans are:
- Pensions
- 401(k)s
- IRAs
- Profit Sharing
- Keoghs
- SEPs
- Money Purchase Plans
- Others[2]

In some states, if you are married, your spouse must sign a written consent before you can name someone else (such as your former spouse or mistress) as your beneficiary.

Life Insurance

Any life insurance policy that you have allows you to designate in writing in advance your beneficiary in the event of your death.[3]

Trusts

A written trust agreement allows you to:
- Appoint a trustee to hold and mange your assets
- Specify the assets you would like to place in a trust
- Name the beneficiaries of your property placed in trust
- Designate when the trust will end[4]

Trust for a Pet

In some states, you can now establish trusts to care for your pets following your death.

Property in Joint Tenancy

If you own property as a joint tenant upon your death, your property is automatically transferred to your surviving joint tenant.

You can have property in joint tenancy for:
- Real estate
- Savings accounts
- Checking accounts
- Stock brokerage accounts

Property that is not titled as a joint tenancy has to be transferred via your will and may be subject to estate and inheritance taxes and other taxes.[5]

Probate

After your death, there is a process called probate that:
- Identifies all your property
- Collects all your property
- Pays taxes related to your property/estate
- Pays debts related to your property/estate

Your property and assets are then distributed in accordance with the instructions you put in your will.[6]

Living Wills

Any mentally competent person 18 or older may prepare in advance written instructions regarding your medical care preferences. These are called advance directives.

Advance directives primarily include two parts:

- **Living Will:** This document spells out the types of medical treatments and life-sustaining measures you do and do not want, such as mechanical respiration and tube feeding. In some states the living will may be known by a different name, such as a health care declaration or health care directive. Via a living will you can provide that you do not want to be kept alive by artificial life support mechanism if you are:
  - Comatose
  - Terminally ill
  - Beyond hope of recovery

- **Medical Power of Attorney (POA)**: Also called a Durable Power of Attorney for health care of a health care agent or proxy, the medical POA form is a legal document that designates an individual to make medical decisions on your behalf in the event you are unable to do so. The medical POA document is different from the power of attorney form that authorizes someone to make financial transactions for you. If you do not appoint a medical POA, the decisions about your care default to your spouse. If you are not legally married, decisions fall to your adult children or your parents.[8]

Intestate Succession

If you do not have a will at your death or your will is not valid, the state you lived in provides by law how your property will be distributed. This is called intestate succession.

Intestate succession is the method by which property is distributed when a person dies without a valid will. Each state's law provides that the property be distributed to the closest surviving relatives. In most states, the surviving spouse, children, parents, siblings, nieces and nephews, and next of kin inherit, in that order.[7]

Financial Power of Attorney

A Financial Power of Attorney document allows you to name another person to act on your behalf for financial and legal matters if you become incapacitated or disabled and cannot make decisions.

If you have the Power of Attorney in place, a court will not have to appoint a conservator to make decisions on your behalf.[9]

Anatomical Gifts

An anatomical gift is a donation of organs and tissues. Advancements in medicine have now made it possible to transplant twenty-five different human organs and tissues, including corneas, heart, liver, kidney, lungs, pancreas, bone, and skin. Donations may also be used for research related to diseases, disabilities, and injuries.

The Uniform Anatomical Gift Act was enacted in August 1968 for the purpose of establishing uniform laws regarding organ and tissue donations. All 50 states and the District of Columbia have adopted the act, with some states making minor variations.

Any individual of sound mind who is at least 18 years of age may execute an anatomical gift either for personal donation or on behalf of another.[10]

Anatomical Gifts

Anatomical Gifts: in many states you can designate yourself as an organ donor on your driver's license in the event of your death.

● ● ● ● ● ● ● ●

NOTES

● ● ● ● ● ● ● ●

CHAPTER ONE

1. Virginia State Bar, "So You're 18: A Handbook on Your Legal Rights and Responsibilities," 2006, page 4.
2. State Bar of Michigan, "You and the Law," 2000, page 13.
3. Illinois State Bar Association, "Becoming an Adult: Your Legal Rights and Responsibilities at Age 18," 2007, page 25.
4. IBID, page 26.
5. www.soundvision.com
6. www.sadd.org
7. www.soundvision.com
8. www.sadd.org
9. www.familyfirstaid.org
10. www.soundvision.org
11. IBID.
12. IBID.
13. www.nationalpost.com
14. www.ananova.com
15. IBID.
16. IBID.
17. www.courtinfo.ca.gov
18. IBID.
19. IBID.
20. IBID.
21. Colorado Bar Association, "So, You're 18 Now: A Survival Guide for Your Adults; Rights and Responsibilities," 2005, page 2.
22. IBID, page 5.
23. IBID, page 2
24. www.parentingteens.about.com

CHAPTER TWO

1. www.abc.com
2. www.answers.com
3. www.statesboroherald.com

4. Colorado Bar Association, "So, You're 18 Now: A Survival Guide for Your Adults; Rights and Responsibilities," 2005, page 23.
5. www.totallawyers.com
6. IBID.
7. www.kubc.com
8. www.tampabays10.com
9. www.stopthedrugwar.com
10. www.latimes.com
11. www.officer.com/web/online
12. California Bar Foundation, "When You Become 18: A Survival Guide for Teenagers," 2008, page 13.
13. Colorado Bar Association, "So, You're 18 Now: A Survival Guide for Your Adults; Rights and Responsibilities," 2005, page 5.
14. Nebraska State Bar Foundation, "Reaching the Age of Majority: Your Legal Rights and Responsibilities," 2006, page 15.
15. www.citmedicalaw.org
16. California Bar Foundation, "When You Become 18: A Survival Guide for Teenagers," 2008, page 11.
17. www.citmedialaw.org

CHAPTER THREE

1. www.shopliftingattorney.com
2. www.azstarnet.com
3. State Bar of Michigan, "You and the Law," 2000, page 20.
4. www.onlinelawyersource.com
5. www.abcnews.go.com
6. www.kidshealth.org
7. www.lacriminaldefenseattorney.com
8. www.breitbart.com

CHAPTER FOUR

1. www.san-francisco-dui.blogspot.com
2. www.usatoday.com
3. State Bar of Michigan, "You and the Law," 2000, pages 17, 18.
4. IBID, page 18.
5. www.boston.com
6. www.neahin.org
7. www.ucanchicago.org
8. *Scottish Daily Mail*, January 27, 2009.

CHAPTER FIVE

1. www.answers.com
2. www.blogsaftety.com
3. www.atlantamagazine.com
4. www.kff.org
5. www.criminallawyers.com
6. www.cnews.canoe.ca/cnews/crime
7. www.lectlaw.com
8. IBID.
9. *Newsweek*, February 23, 2009.
10. www.boston.com
11. *USA Today*, March 13, 2009.
12. California Bar Foundation, "When You Become 18: A Survival Guide for Teenagers," 2008, page 8.
13. www.teenadvice.about.com
14. www.4woman.gov
15. www.ncvc.org
16. www.duhamie.org
17. www.missthemess.com
18. www.ncvc.org
19. IBID.
20. www.missthemess.com
21. *Teen Sex and Pregnancy*, The Alan Guttmacher Institute, New York, 1996.
22. www.troubledteen101.com
23. www.duhamie.com

24. www.npr.org
25. www.acadv.org/dating
26. IBID.
27. IBID.
28. IBID.
29. IBID.
30. IBID.
31. www.duhamie.org

CHAPTER SIX

1. Maine State Bar Association, "On Your Own," 2009, page 12.
2. IBID.
3. www.teenfi.com
4. www.usatoday.com
5. www.ncvc.org
6. www.bangornews.org
7. Talking Resource Center, *The National Center for Victims of Crime. Stalking Fact Sheet*, www.ncvc.org
8. Fisher, Bonnie, et al, U.S. Department of Justice, NCJ 182369, *The Sexual Victimization of College Women*, 2000.
9. www.womenissues.about.com
10. www.socialsafety.org
11. www.symantec.com
12. IBID.
13. www.ajc.com
14. www.i.gizmodo.com

CHAPTER SEVEN

1. www.answers.com
2. www.wlfi.com
3. www.newser.com
4. www.startelegram.typepad.com
5. www.wesh.com
6. www.nytimes.com
7. www.theglobeandmail.com

CHAPTER EIGHT

1. www.todaysthv.com
2. www.earthtimes.org
3. www.preferredconsumer.com
4. www.wikipedia.com
5. www.cnylink.com
6. www.drugrehabs.org
7. www.kywlogo.com
8. www.ghsa.org
9. www.sadd.org
10. www.accidents.com
11. www.idfpr.com
12. Maine State Bar Association, "On Your Own," 2009, page 36.
13. *Newsweek*, May 14, 2007.
14. *USAToday*, January 17, 2008.
15. www.idfpr.com
16. www.myfoxdfw.com
17. www.blogs.chron.com

CHAPTER NINE

1. California Bar Foundation, "When You Become 18: A Survival Guide for Teenagers," 2008, pages 4, 5.
2. www.krld.com
3. www.marquee.fsu.edu.
4. www.sowal.com
5. www.marquee.fsu.edu.
6. www.nytimes.com
7. www.family.samhsa.gov
8. IBID.
9. www.thestar.co.za.
10. www.tallahassee.com

CHAPTER TEN

1. City of Hamilton, Ontario.
2. www.poconorecord.com
3. www.sanantonio.gov
4. www.caller.com
5. www.silive.com

CHAPTER ELEVEN

1. Nebraska State Bar Foundation, "Reaching the Age of Majority: Your Legal Rights and Responsibilities," 2006, page 2.
2. www.wcbs880.com
3. www.umadd.org
4. www.bradycampaign.org
5. U.S. Surgeon General, 1991.
6. www.sadd.org
7. State Bar of Michigan, "You and the Law," 2000, page 7.
8. www.familyfirstaid.org
9. www.sadd.org
10. www.soundvision.com
11. www.quitsmoking.about.com
12. IBID.
13. www.soundvision.com
14. California Bar Foundation, "When You Become 18: A Survival Guide for Teenagers," 2008, page 5.
15. www.podango.com
16. www.dumbcriminals.com
17. www.sadd.org
18. www.ojp.usdoj.gov
19. www.independentsources.com
20. www.altenet.org
21. www.cnn.com
22. www.teenoverthecounterdrugabuse.com
23. www.teendrugabuse.us/prescription_drug_abuse.html
24. IBID.
25. IBID.
26. www.ojp.usdoj.gov

CHAPTER TWELVE

1. www.seattletimes.nwsource.com
2. www.findarticles.com
3. www.dmv.org
4. www.wcbstv.com
5. Virginia State Bar, "So You're 18: A Handbook on Your Legal Rights and Responsibilities," 2006, page 12.
6. December 1, 2006, KTHV, Little Rock.
7. www.ananova.com
8. www.wftv.com/automotive

CHAPTER THIRTEEN

1. www.cmgesq.com
2. State Bar of Michigan, "You and the Law," 2000, page 22.
3. www.usdoj.gov
4. www.eureaclert.org
5. www.kidshealth.org
6. www.usdoj.gov

CHAPTER FOURTEEN

1. Maine State Bar Association, "On Your Own," 2009, page 7.
2. IBID.
3. IBID.
4. www.ftc.gov
5. IBID.
6. IBID.
7. IBID.
8. www.arlingtonva.us/departments
9. IBID.

CHAPTER FIFTEEN

1. www.jobsearch.about.com
2. U.S. Department of Labor.
3. Truly, Traci, *Teen Rights, a Legal Guide for Teens and the Adults in Their Lives*, Sphinx Publishing, 2002, page 181.
4. IBID, page 181.
5. IBID, page 182.
6. www.usatoday.com
7. www.wikipedia.com
8. Truly, Traci, *Teen Rights, a Legal Guide for Teens and the Adults in Their Lives*, Sphinx Publishing, 2002, page 182.
9. www.dol.gov
10. Maine State Bar Association, "On Your Own," 2009, page 9.
11. www.about.com
12. www.worker-comp-law.com
13. www.ojp.usdoj.gov
14. Maine State Bar Association, "On Your Own," 2009, page 11.
15. www.jobsearchtech.about.com
16. IBID.
17. Texas Department of Insurance.
18. IBID.

CHAPTER SIXTEEN

1. www.ftc.gov
2. IBID.
3. www.dmv.org
4. IBID.
5. IBID.
6. www.carbuyingtips.com
7. www.dmv.org
8. www.autorepair.ca.gov
9. IBID.
10. Maine State Bar Association, "On Your Own," 2009, page 34.
11. www.fraudguides.com
12. IBID.
13. www.personalinsure.com
14. www.idfpr.com
15. Maine State Bar Association, "On Your Own," 2009, page 36.
16. IBID.
17. IBID, page 33.
18. www.dmv.org

CHAPTER SEVENTEEN

1. Iowa State Bar Association, "On Your Own: Your Legal Rights and Responsibilities as an Adult," 2005, page 14.
2. IBID.
3. www.totallyuselessknowledge.com
4. Iowa State Bar Association, "On Your Own: Your Legal Rights and Responsibilities as an Adult," 2005, page 14.
5. Vermont Bar Association, "On Your Own: Your Legal Rights at 18," 2004, pages 36, 37.
6. www.completelandlord.com
7. IBID.
8. www.aba.net.org

CHAPTER EIGHTEEN

1. www.wikipedia.com
2. www.freeadvice.com
3. www.blogs.kansascity.com
4. www.totallyuselessknowledge.com
5. www.cbsnews.com
6. www.freeadvice.com
7. IBID.
8. www.totallyuselessknowledge.com
9. www.newciv.org
10. www.wikipedia.com
11. www.ncpa.org
12. www.associatedcontent.com
13. Colorado Bar Association, "So, You're 18 NowL: A Survival Guide for Your Adults; Rights and Responsibilities," 2005, page 11.
14. www.totallyuselessknowledge.com
15. www.bbc.co.uk.

16. California Bar Foundation, "When You Become 18: A Survival Guide for Teenagers," 2008, page 10.
17. IBID.
18. Colorado Bar Association, "So, You're 18 Now: A Survival Guide for Your Adults; Rights and Responsibilities," 2005, pages 12, 13.
19. California Bar Foundation, "When You Become 18: A Survival Guide for Teenagers," 2008, page 10.
20. www.totallyuselssknowledge.com
21. IBID.
22. www.evanslegal.com
23. www.divorcesupport.com
24. Iowa State Bar Association, "On Your Own: Your Legal Rights and Responsibilities as an Adult," 2005, pages 9, 10.
25. Jaden, Patricia T. and Nancy Thoennes. U.S. Department of Justice, NCJ 183781. *Full Report of the Prevalence, Incidences and Consequences of Intimate Partner Violence Against Women: Findings From The National Violence Against Women Survey,* 2000.
26. Rennison, Callie Marie. U. S. Department of Justice, NCJ 197838. "Bureau of Justice Statistic Crime Data Brief: Intimate Partner Violence," 1993-2001.
27. Maine State Bar Association, "On Your Own," 2009, page 15.
28. IBID.
29. IBID.

CHAPTER NINETEEN

1. www.co.jefferson.co.us/sheriff.com
2. www.ftc.gov
3. www.newsobserver.com
4. www.int.comarticles.
5. www.sans.org
6. www.co.jefferson.co.us/sheriff.com
7. Vermont Bar Association, "On Your Own: Your Legal Rights at 18," 2004, pages 48-49.
8. www.softpedia.com
9. www.pcworld.com
10. Vermont Bar Association, "On Your Own: Your Legal Rights at 18," 2004, pages 47, 48.
11. www.crime-research.org
12. www.healthtribune.com
13. www.news.bbc.co.uk.
14. California Bar Foundation, "When You Become 18: A Survival Guide for Teenagers," 2008, page 14.
15. www.sflu.org
16. www.netfamilynews.org

17. www.scholar.lib.vt.edu.
18. www.jointogether.org
19. www.arlingtonva.us/departments.
20. www.crime-research.org
21. www.ftc.gov
22. www.nydailynews.com

CHAPTER TWENTY

1. State Bar of Wisconsin, "On Being 18," 2006, page 23.
2. California Bar Foundation, "When You Become 18: A Survival Guide for Teenagers," 2008, page 6.
3. www.ftc.gov
4. www.ezinearticles.com
5. www.debtfreedestiny.com
6. www.ftc.gov
7. Virginia State Bar, "So You're 18: A Handbook on Your Legal Rights and Responsibilities," 2006, page 22.
8. State Bar of Wisconsin, "On Being 18," 2006, page 20.

CHAPTER TWENTY-ONE

1. Colorado Bar Association, "So, You're 18 Now: A Survival Guide for Your Adults; Rights and Responsibilities," 2005, page 17.
2. IBID, pages 17, 18.
3. IBID, page 18.
4. IBID.
5. IBID.
6. IBID.
7. www.nolo.com
8. www.mayoclinic.com
9. Colorado Bar Association, "So, You're 18 Now: A Survival Guide for Your Adults; Rights and Responsibilities," 2005, page 19.
10. www.mobar.org

INDEX

● ● ● ● ● ● ● ●